Dhyan Manik

Learning Thai
with
hâi ให้

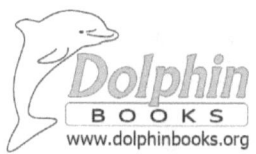

22 Secrets *of* Learning Thai

Copyright © Dhyan Manik and Dolphin Books 2016

First printing 2016, Second printing 2020

Cover design and layout: Uri Hautamäki / Data Graphics, Helsinki

Pictures: of hâi ให้: Tone Artist

> Audio spoken in MP3 format by native speakers can be loaded from the following address:
>
> www.thaibooks.net
>
> Thai voice: Ms. Waree Singhanart
>
> English voice: Mr. Mark Harris

Publisher:

Dolphin Books

info@dolphinbooks.org

www.dolphinbooks.org

ISBN 978-9526651156

Acknowledgement

I would like to thank the following people for giving their time and energy to help me to write this book.

First of all, I would like to thank Ms. Waree Singhanart, a Thai Teacher from Bangkok, for looking over the book with me. She has helped me a great deal with choosing the correct Thai sentences and proofreading the Thai text.

Ms. Duangmon Loprakhong, a Thai teacher from Bangkok, has helped me with checking the Thai syntax and given advice on the special grammar and usage of the word hâi ให้.

Ms. Kamolthip Jitpattanakul, Academic Services Center, Faculty of Arts, Intensive Thai, Chulalongkorn University, Bangkok, has given me valuable advice on structural aspects of how Thai people use the word hâi ให้ in everyday speech.

Mr. Watit Pumyoo, Department of Thai, Chiang Mai University, has given me guidence on the Thai writing system and semantic aspects of the word hâi ให้. He has also significantly improved the phonetic descriptions of the Thai words.

Mr. Mark Harris, has read the book and suggested various amendments to improve the clarity and style of the written English.

I also want to thank Mr. Walter Kassela, who has proofread the book and pointed out several changes regarding the syntax and linguistic aspects of the English language.

Lastly, I want to thank everybody who is interested in reading this book and learning Thai.

Table of Contents

Introduction 13
A Thai girl called **hâi** ให้ 15
Transliteration and translation 15
Grammatical terms used in this book 16
Meeting with **hâi** 19

Part I – hâi ให้ *to give* as a main verb

Secret 1 – hâi ให้ *to give* **something to someone** 23
   A. Sentences with: **hâi-ngən** ให้ เงิน *to give money*
      – **hâi-aahăan** ให้ อาหาร *to give food*
      – **hâi-tŭua** ให้ ตั๋ว *to give a ticket* 24
   B. Understanding hâi ให้ and giving something to someone 26
      – the basic usage of hâi ให้ as *to give something to someone*
   C. Language hints 28
      – changing the meaning of hâi ให้ into *to let* in English
   D. Simple advice 30
      – the importance of the word order

Secret 2 – hâi ให้ *to give* **something to someone with kàp** กับ **or kɛ̀ɛ** แก่ 33
   A. Sentences with: **kàp** กับ and **kɛ̀ɛ** แก่ 34
   B. Understanding hâi with **kàp** กับ and **kɛ̀ɛ** แก่ 37
      – **kàp** กับ and **kɛ̀ɛ** แก่ with classifiers
   C. Language hints 38
      – understanding Thai classifiers
   D. Simple advice 40
      – English measure words vs. Thai classifiers

Secret 3 – hâi ให้ changing nouns into verbs 43
   A. Sentences with: **hâi-sìt** ให้ สิทธิ์ *to authorize*
      – **hâi-thâa** ให้ ท่า *to flirt*
      – **hâi-àphai** ให้ อภัย *to forgive* 44
   B. Understanding hâi ให้ and making nouns become verbs 46
      – changing abstract nouns into verbs with hâi ให้
   C. Language hints 48
      – examples of Thai loan words
   D. Simple advice 49
      – the importance of the context when speaking Thai

Part II – hâi ให้ as a causative verb

Secret 4 – hâi ให้ as a causative main verb, *to let, to request, to order* 53
   A. Sentences with: **hâi** ให้ *to let*
      – **hâi** ให้ *to request*
      – **hâi** ให้ *to order* 54
   B. Understanding **hâi** ให้ as a causative verb 58
      – *to let, to request, to order* are expressed with the single word hâi ให้
   C. Language hints 59
      – using hâi ให้ intuitively
   D. Simple advice 61
      – hâi ให้ as *to cause* or *to make* someone else to do something

Secret 5 – hâi ให้ as a causative compound verb for *making* something happen 65
   A. Sentences with: **tham-hâi** ทำ ให้ *to make*
      – **tʃûuai-hâi** ช่วย ให้ *to help* 66
   B. Understanding hâi ให้ as a causative compound verb for *making* something happen 68
      – hâi ให้ as a second element in the compound verb for *making* something happen
   C. Language hints 69
      – two most common prefixes in Thai,
   khwaam ความ *matter* and **kaan** การ *task*
   D. Simple advice 72
      – importance of being more concerned with *how* rather than with *why*

Secret 6 – hâi ให้ as a causative compound verb for *allowing* 75
   A. Sentences with: **yɔɔm-hâi** ยอม ให้ *to allow*
      – **ànúyâat-hâi** อนุญาต ให้ *to permit*
      – **plɔ̀ɔi-hâi** ปล่อย ให้ *to release* 76
   B. Understanding **hâi** ให้ as a causative compound verb *for allowing* 78
      – **hâi** ให้ as a second element in the compound verb *to allow, to permit, to release*
   C. Language hints 80
      – using **yɔɔm** ยอม *to allow*
      – **ànúyâat** อนุญาต *to permit*
      – **plɔ̀ɔi** ปล่อย ให้ *to release* alone without **hâi** ให้
   D. Simple advice 83
      – importance of learning the correct structure of the Thai language

Secret 7 – hâi ให้ as a causative compound verb for *making a request* 85
   A. Sentences with: **yàak-hâi** อยาก ให้ *to want to*
      – **tôngˈ-gaan-hâi** ต้อง การ ให้ *to want to*
      – **yàak-dâai** อยาก ได้ *to want to get*
      – **au** เอา, *to want, to take* 86
   B. Understanding **hâi** ให้ as a causative compound verb
      for *making a request* 89
      – **hâi** ให้ as a second element in the compound verb for *making a request*
   C. Language hints 92
      – different ways to translate the English verb *to want* into Thai
   D. Simple advice 98
      – the difference between expressions: *general wanting, would like to* and *stating a request*

Secret 8 – hâi ให้ as a causative compound verb for *firm ordering* 101
   A. Sentences with: **sàng-hâi** สั่ง ให้ *to order*
      – **tɔ̂ng-hâi** ต้อง ให้ *must*
      – **bɔ̀ɔk-hâi** บอก ให้ *to tell*
      – **rîiak-hâi** เรียก ให้ *to call* 102
   B. Understanding **hâi** ให้ as a causative compound verb for giving
      orders 105
      – **hâi** ให้ as a second element in the compound verb for *giving orders*
   C. Language hints 107
      – using the verb **sàng** สั่ง *to order* alone without **hâi** ให้
   D. Simple advice 111
      – importance of learning the Thai language from phrases and sentences rather than from single words

Secret 9 – hâi ให้ and some special verbs 113
   A. Sentences with: **hâi-yɯɯm** ให้ ยืม *to lend, to borrow*
      – **hâi-rúu** ให้รู้ *to let know*
      – **hâi-duu** ให้ ดู *to let look* 114
   B. Understanding hâi ให้ and some special verbs 116
      – using hâi ให้ as a first element in a compound *structure*
   C. Language hints 117
      – understanding hâi ให้ *to let* and hâi ให้ *to give*
   D. Simple advice 121
      – more on the meanings of hâi ให้ *to give*

Part III – hâi ให้ and offering help and being polite

Secret 10 – hâi ให้ and offering help 125
   A. Sentences with: **hâi-tʃán-tʃûuai** ให้ ฉัน ช่วย *let me help you*
      – **hâi-tʃán-tham-hâi** ให้ ฉัน ทำ ให้ *let me do it for you* 126
   B. Understanding hâi ให้ and offering help 128
      – the word order for offering help with hâi ให้
   C. Language hints 129
      – polite ways to reply when offered help
   D. Simple advice 130
      – improving your language skills and identifying your weak points

Secret 11 – hâi ให้ and being polite 133
   A. Sentences with: **khɔ̌ɔ-hâi**... ná khá ขอ ให้... นะ คะ *polite asking*
      – **yàak-hâi**... nɔ̀i dâai-mǎi อยาก ให้... หน่อย ได้ ไหม *polite wanting*
      – **bɔ̀ɔk-hâi**... dûuai ná khá บอก ให้... ด้วย นะ คะ *polite telling* 134
   B. Understanding hâi ให้ and being polite 136
      – hâi ให้ as a second element in the compound verb when *being polite*
      – softening the request by request particles, such as **ná khá**
   นะ คะ for women and **khráp** ครับ for men
   C. Language hints 139
      – the polite request particles at the end of the sentence (**khâ** ค่ะ for women, **khráp** ครับ for men, **nɔ̀i-dâai-mǎi** หน่อย ได้ ไหม could you, please.)
   D. Simple advice 140
      – learning to use polite request particles

Secret 12 – hâi ให้ and to persuade, to ask, to invite 143
   A. Sentences with: **tʃuuan-hâi** ชวน ให้ *to persuade*
      – **khɔ̌ɔ-hâi** ขอ ให้ *to ask*
      – **tʃəən-hâi** เชิญ ให้ *to invite* 144

B. Understanding **hâi** ให้ and persuading someone to do something 146
 – **hâi** ให้ as a second element in the compound verb for persuading
 – **tʃuuan-hâi** ชวน ให้ *to persuade* is quite demanding
 – **khɔ̌ɔ-hâi** ขอ ให้ *to ask* can be used in many situations
 – **tʃəən-hâi** ชวน ให้ *to invite* is used in formal situations only

C. Language hints 148
 – polite request particles **nɔ̀i** หน่อย little, **dûuai** ด้วย also, **dâai-mǎi** ได้ ไหม can you?, **khâ** ค่ะ polite particle for women, **khráp** ครับ polite particle for men, **ná** นะ ok?

D. Simple advice 150
 – handy expression **khɔ̌ɔ-hâi** ขอ ให้ *to ask* can be used in many different situations

Part IV – hâi ให้ before pronouns, adjectives and adverbs

Secret 13 – **hâi** ให้ **as a preposition** *for* – *for you, for me* 155
 A. Sentences with: **hâi-kháu** ให้ เขา *for him*
 – **hâi-khun** ให้ คุณ *for you*
 – **hâi-thúk-khon** ให้ ทุก คน *for everybody* 156
 B. Understanding **hâi** ให้ as a preposition *for* 158
 – **hâi** ให้ as a preposition *for* before a personal pronoun
 C. Language hints 160
 – more ways to express the English words *for* or *to*
 D. Simple advice 163
 – practising, repeating and understanding the structure of the Thai language

Secret 14 – **hâi** ให้ **before adjectives** 167
 A. Sentences with: **hâi-sǔuai** เขียน ให้ สวย *beautifully*
 – **hâi-dii** ให้ ดี *well, nicely*
 – **hâi-thùuk-tɔ̂ng** ให้ ถูก ต้อง *correctly* 168
 B. Understanding **hâi** ให้ before adjectives 170
 – placing **hâi** ให้ before an adjective converts the adjective into an adverb
 C. Language hints 172
 – more ways to make adjectives become adverbs
 D. Simple advice 174
 – **hâi** ให้ and the simple basic sentence

Secret 15 – hâi ให้ before adverbs 177
   A. Sentences with: **hâi-glai** ให้ ไกล *far away*
      – **hâi-thûua** ให้ ทั่ว *everywhere*
      – **hâi-naan-naan** ให้ นานๆ *very long time* 178
   B. Understanding hâi ให้ before adverbs 180
      – hâi ให้ before an adverb tells more about the action in question
   C. Language hints 181
      – hâi ให้ before nouns, personal pronouns, adjectives and adverbs expressing different meanings
   D. Simple advice 184
      – the need to pronounce Thai vowels clearly short or long

Secret 16 – hâi ให้ as *until* 187
   A. Sentences with: **hâi-thǔng** ให้ ถึง *until arriving*
      – **hâi-maa** ให้ มา *until I come*
      – **hâi-tem** ให้ เต็ม *until full* 188
   B. Understanding hâi ให้ as *until* 190
      – hâi ให้ translated into English as *until* in front of *nouns, pronouns* or *verbs*
   C. Language hints 192
      – other ways to express the English word *until* in Thai
   D. Simple advice 193
      – thinking as Thai people do when using the verb hâi ให้

Secret 17 – hâi ให้ in idiomatic expressions 195
   A. Sentences with: **pai-hâi-phón** ไป ให้ พ้น *Leave me alone! Go away!*
      – **hâi-dâai** ให้ ได้ *Whatever happens!*
      – **plɔ̀ɔi-hâi-pen-pai** ปล่อย ให้ เป็น ไป *Let it be!*
      – **hâi-taai** ให้ ตาย *Damn it!* 196
   B. Understanding hâi ให้ in idiomatic expressions 198
      – hâi ให้ in central role in many idiomatic expressions
   C. Language hints 199
      – special ways to use idiomatic expressions
   D. Simple advice 201
      – having fun when using idiomatic expressions

Part V – More practice with hâi ให้

Secret 18 – hâi ให้ between two verbs 205
   A. Sentences with **sàdɛɛng-hâi-hěn** แสดง ให้ เห็น *to show, to indicate*
      – **bɔ̀ɔk-hâi-rúu** บอก ให้ รู้ *to tell, to let know*
      – **tsɛ̂ɛng-hâi-sâap** แจ้ง ให้ ทราบ *to inform, to announce* 206

B. Understanding **hâi** ให้ between two verbs 208
   – hâi ให้ between two verbs, strong and clear meaning
C. Language hints 210
   – more examples, hâi ให้ between two verbs
D. Simple advice 212
   – using the right word in the right situation

Secret 19 – hâi ให้ and questions 215
A. Sentences with: **dâai-mái** ได้ ไหม *can I* -question
   – **mái** ไหม *question word*
   – **rʉ́-plàau** รึ เปล่า *or not* -question
   – **khrai** ใคร *who-question* 216
B. Understanding hâi ให้ and questions 221
   – learning to use question words correctly
C. Language hints 222
   – question words either at the end or at the beginning of the sentence
D. Simple advice 227
   – the rule of using **kìi** กี่ *how many* correctly

Secret 20 – hâi ให้ and negatives statements 229
A. Sentences with: **mâi-yàak-hâi** ไม่ อยาก ให้ *do not want*
   – **mâi-hâi** ไม่ ให้ *will not let*
   – hâi ให้ and **mâi-dâai** ไม่ ได้ *cannot* 230
B. Understanding hâi ให้ and negative statements 232
   – **mâi** ไม่ *no* and **yàa** อย่า *do not* with hâi ให้
C. Language hints 234
   – several more words for negative expressions
D. Simple advice 237
   – making negative statements sound more positive

Secret 21 – hâi ให้ several times in one statement 241
A. Sentences with: **hâi khun... hâi tʃǎn** ให้ คุณ... ให้ ฉัน *you... for me*
   – **tsɛ̂ɛng-hâi-sâap... hâi thúk-khon** แจ้ง ให้ ทราบ... ให้ ทุก คน *to inform... everybody*
   – **hâi khun... tham-hâi... hâi-dii** ให้ คุณ... ทำ ให้... ให้ ดี *to you... to make... well* 242
B. Understanding hâi ให้ in different roles in one sentence 245
   – hâi ให้ appearing several times in one sentence with different meanings
C. Language hints 246
   – summarising the usage of the word hâi ให้
D. Simple advice 251
   – four simple ways to use the word hâi ให้

Secret 22 – hâi ให้ and changing the word order 253
   A. Sentences with **khɔ̌ɔ-khun-hâi** ขอ คุณ ให้ *to ask you to*
      – **bɔ̀ɔk-kháu-hâi** บอก เขา ให้ *to tell him*
      – **tɯɯan-thúk-khon-hâi** เตือน ทุก คน ให้ *to warn everybody* 254
   B. Understanding **hâi** ให้ and changing the word order 257
      – **hâi** ให้ before or after the personal pronoun
      – **khɔ̌ɔ-khun-hâi** ขอ คุณ ให้ or **khɔ̌ɔ-hâi-khun** ขอ ให้ คุณ *to ask you to*
   C. Language hints 258
      – changing the word order or not
   D. Simple advice 262
      – using the word order **khɔ̌ɔ-hâi-khun** ขอ ให้ คุณ *to ask you to,* **hâi** ให้ before the personal pronoun is right with all verbs

Part VI – Introduction to Thai sounds and some useful grammar terms

A. Introduction to sounds and Thai transliteration 264
1. Thai consonant sounds 265
   1.1 Stop consonant sounds
      1.1.1 Aspirated stop consonants
      1.1.2 Unaspirated stop consonants
      1.1.3 Affricate stop consonants
      1.1.4 Voiced stop consonants
   1.2 Fricative consonant sounds
   1.3 Sonorant consonant sounds
2. Thai vowel sounds – long and short 273

B. Summary of some useful grammar terms 282
1. Grammar 282
   1.1 Phonetics
   1.2 Transliteration
   1.3 Syntax
   1.4 Semantics
   1.5 Semantic boundary
2. Parts of speech 283
   2.1 Nouns
      2.1.1 Common nouns
      2.1.2 Abstract nouns
      2.1.3 Classifiers

  2.2 Personal pronouns
  2.3 Verbs
    2.3.1 Main verb
    2.3.2 Helping verb
    2.3.3 Action verbs
    2.3.4 State verbs
    2.3.5 Causative verbs
    2.3.6 Causative compound verbs
  2.4. Adjectives
    2.4.1 Adjectives as adjectives
    2.4.2 Adjectives as verbs
    2.4.3 Adjectives as adverbs
  2.5 Adverbs
    2.5.1 Adverbs of time
    2.5.2 Adverbs of frequency
    2.5.3 Adverbs of place
  2.6. Prepositions
  2.7 Conjunctions
3. Making sentences..287
  3.1 Simple subject
  3.2 Simple predicate
  3.3 Object
    3.3.1 Direct object
    3.3.2 Indirect object
  3.4 Subject-verb-object in the sentence
  3.5 Tenses
  3.6 Time aspect
  3.7 Context
  3.8 Short form
  3.9 Idiomatic expressions
  3.10 Gerund
  3.11 Genitive/possessive case
  3.12 Polite particles
4. Other terms... 289
  4 .1 Schwa

Learning Thai with hâi ให้

Introduction

How to use the verb **hâi** ให้

hâi ให้, along with words like dâai ได้ lɛ́ɛu แล้ว and kɔ̂ɔ ก็, is one of the most important words in the Thai language.

Thai people use the verb **hâi** ให้ regularly in daily situations in many different ways. Unless you know how to use this word well, your Thai is lacking something essential.

While speaking Thai one needs to understand how the verb **hâi** ให้ is used correctly as Thai people do in everyday speech.

Speaking a language is a skill like any other skill. It does not matter whether it is your own language or a second language. When learning a second language like Thai it is good to understand the structural differences in relation to your own language. It is only natural to try to impose the structure of your own language onto Thai. However, the grammar and the way ideas are expressed in Thai is very different from English or any other major western language.

> Therefore, it would be very beneficial to your language studies to understand the grammatical mechanisms of the Thai language. It relies very much on the syntactic structure of the language based on word order. In Thai, all words are in basic form. That means that words are not declined or inflected in any manner. For example, there are no tenses, no genders and no plural forms in Thai.

Because of this, some people may think that the Thai language is simple, inexplicit and has no grammar. Such presumptions are far from the truth. Thai uses a different mechanism to express ideas. Every language is unique, and the things that make the Thai language unique allow you to express ideas precisely and implicitly. The structures and mechanisms that Thai uses to do this are different from those used in English.

For Thai people **hâi** ให้ is a single word, and they don't think of it having different semantic meanings. However, the translation into English differs considerably depending on where it stands in the sentence, how the statement is said, and what other words are used with it.

> One simple way to use the verb hâi ให้ is *to give* something to someone. It is used in a similar way as the verb *to give* is used in English. The word order in Thai is often different, however.

In addition, **hâi** ให้ is used as *a causative verb* with several different meanings depending on the situation, and the way it is spoken. It can be translated into English as *to cause, to make, to let, to allow,* and even *to order* or *to force* someone to do something.

In some situations **hâi** ให้ is better translated into English as a preposition *"for"*, as in *"for you"*, *"for me"*. It is also often used in idiomatic phrases where it carries no meaning itself but denotes only a sense of a command.

> Thais use the verb hâi ให้ in an intuitive way in a variety of situations in order to express feelings, wishes, commands, and particular nuances while communicating with each other every day. If you learn this word well you will be rewarded.

A Thai girl called hâi ให้

We have decided to give the verb **hâi** ให้ a face and a name to make her a young Thai girl, **Hâi** ให้. That way the verb **hâi** ให้ becomes more lively, learning becomes a bit more fun and perhaps also easier. Most Thai girls have a nickname and usually this is given by their mother. In real life **Hâi** ให้ is not a common nickname.

In our book **Hâi** ให้ is pictured as a cute and sincere young Thai girl. She can adapt herself very easily and plays several major and minor roles while interacting with other people.

In order to understand her fully, some sensitivity is needed from you. She's not, however, a complicated person, and is always ready to help you and to find new ways to approach life. She is a lot of fun.

> In this book we are learning Thai with hâi ให้. Hence, the "Language hints" in section C. and the "Simple advice" in section D. contain notes on Thai language and grammar, which go beyond the usage of the verb hâi ให้. These can be more general in nature.

Enjoy **hâi** ให้ and all 22 Secrets.

Transliteration and translation

> You would be well advised to get yourself acquainted with basic phonetics and Thai sounds, and how they are produced and transliterated. You will then find that learning Thai becomes much easier. To understand some basic phonetics does not apply only to Thai, but other languages as well. After all almost all English dictionaries contain phonetic symbols.
>
> A short presentation of Thai sounds, transliteration and phonetics is given at the end of this book.

When we translate sentences in this book, we give two different translations. First, the correct English translation of the overall sense of the meaning conveyed by the Thai phrase or sentence. Then the basic form: a literal word for word translation. Using this method you are hopefully able to follow the structure of the Thai language better. It may also help you to learn new words more easily.

In Thai script words and sentences are usually written together without any spaces. We use spaces between the words in this book since it will be easier for the learner to identify individual written Thai words.

Spaces between words in Thai are used instead of full stops and commas as in English. Otherwise words are written together without any spaces. Since we have decided to put spaces between the words in order to help you to read Thai, we use the symbol (-) when necessary to clarify the meaning of the Thai sentence where English would use a comma or a full stop.

Grammatical terms used in this book

The aim of this book is to teach you how the Thai word **hâi** ให้ is used with other words in sentences. Whether this usage is called grammar, syntax, sentence structure or the Thai way, does not matter. Yet, it is beneficial for us to know some grammatical terms used in English in order to understand the verb **hâi** ให้ and the Thai language.

The grammatical terms chosen in this book are from the perspective of the Thai language. They are not, by any means, an attempt to describe the English grammar. We just need some terms to illustrate how words are put together in Thai and where they are placed in the sentence. We must use the English language in order to understand the structure and the syntax of the Thai language.

The native speakers of any language are not usually aware of the syntax or the structure of their own language. Yet, they are able to make grammatically correct sentences since they are born into the habit of using the correct language. They have absorbed the grammatical rules of their own language subconsciously while learning it as a child.

> You may find it helpful to have a glance at the summary of the grammar terms at the end of this book.

My name is hâi
ฉัน ชื่อ ให้
tʃán tʃɯ̂ɯ hâi

Meeting with hâi

Welcome to the world of hâi

ยิน ดี ต้อน รับ เข้า สู่ โลก ของ ให้

yin-dii tɔ̂ɔn-ráp khâu sùu lôok khɔ̌ɔng hâi

hâi says: "Hello! My name is hâi. hâi is my nickname given to me by my mother. I have eyes, ears and feelings. I am smart, and I can teach you Thai."

ให้ บอก ว่า สวัสดี ค่ะ ฉัน ชื่อ ให้ – ให้ เป็น ชื่อ เล่น ที่ แม่ ตั้ง ให้ ฉัน – ฉัน มี ตา มี หู มี ความ รู้ สึก ฉัน เก่ง และ สอน ภาษา ไทย ให้ คุณ ได้

hâi bɔ̀ɔk-wâa – sàwàtdii khâ tʃǎn tʃɯ̂ɯ hâi – hâi pen tʃɯ̂ɯ-lên thîi mɛ̂ɛ tâng hâi tʃǎn – tʃǎn mii taa mii hǔu mii khwaam-ruu-sùk – tʃǎn kèng lɛ́ sɔ̌ɔn phaasǎa thai hâi khun dâai

hello! I name hâi – hâi is name-play that mother set give I – I have eye have ear have matter-know-consciousness – I diligent and teach language Thai you can

PART I
hâi ให้ *to give* as a main verb

To give money
ให้ เงิน
hâi ngən

> hâi likes to give everything from her heart – hâi says: "I want to give you happiness."
>
> ให้ ชอบ ให้ ทุก สิ่ง ทุก อย่าง จาก ใจ – ให้ บอก ว่า – ฉัน อยาก ให้ ความ สุข กับ คุณ
>
> hâi tʃɔ̌ɔp hâi thúk-sìng-thúk-yàang tsàak tsai – hâi bɔ̀ɔk wâa – tʃǎn yàak-hâi khwaam-sùk kàp khun
>
> hâi like give every-thing-every-kind from heart – hâi tell that – I want-give matter-happy with you

SECRET 1

hâi ให้ *to give* as a main verb

One way to use **hâi** ให้ as a main verb is when it means *to give* something to someone. **hâi** ให้ is placed before the direct object *that is given*.

A. Sentences

To give something to someone

Below we show first the complete sentence and then the short form. The short form is usually used when speaking. The rest of the meaning is understood from the context.

Thais usually like to cut sentences short and use the short form whenever possible.

> **1** To give money – hâi ngən ให้ เงิน
> Mother gave me money to go to school.
> แม่ ให้ เงิน ฉัน ไป โรง เรียน
> mɛ̂ɛ *hâi-ngən-tʃán* pai roong-riian
> mother *give-money-I* go building-study

- **hâi-ngən** ให้ เงิน *to give money*
- **hâi** ให้ *to give* as a main verb is put before the direct object that is given, here **ngən** เงิน *money*
- the indirect object to whom the object is given, here **tʃán** ฉัน *I*, comes after
- the second part of the sentence explains here why the money was given
- the word order is very important
- that which is given comes first, and to whom the object is given comes after

> **Short form**
> แม่ ให้ เงิน ไป โรง เรียน
> mɛ̂ɛ *hâi-ngən* pai roong-riian
> mother *give-money* go building-study

Secret 1 – hâi ให้ *to give* as a main verb

- the indirect object, to whom the object was given, **tʃán** ฉัน *I*, can be omitted when it is understood from the context

> **2** To give food – hâi aahăan ให้ อาหาร
>
> They gave me extra food.
>
> พวก เขา ให้ อาหาร ฉัน เพิ่ม
> phûuak-kháu *hâi-aahăan-tʃán* phə̂ə m
> group-he *give-food-I* extra

- **hâi-aahăan** ให้ อาหาร *to give food, to feed*
- **hâi** ให้ *to give* as a main verb is put before the direct object that is given, here **aahăan** อาหาร *food*
- the indirect object to whom the object is given, here **tʃán** ฉัน, *I* comes after
- note that **hâi-aahăan** ให้ อาหาร *to give food* in Thai is often used as an English verb *to feed* animals

Short form

พวก เขา ให้ อาหาร เพิ่ม
phûuak-kháu *hâi-aahăan* phə̂ə m
group-he *give-food* extra

- the indirect object to whom the object is given, here **tʃán** ฉัน, can be omitted if it is understood from the context

> **3** To give a ticket – hâi tŭua ให้ ตั๋ว
>
> He gave us a ticket to go to Chiang Mai.
>
> เขา ให้ ตั๋ว เรา ไป เชียงใหม่
> kháu *hâi-tŭua-rau* pai tʃiiang-mài
> he *give-ticket-we* go Chiang Mai

- **hâi-tŭua** ให้ ตั๋ว *to give a ticket*
- **hâi** ให้ *to give* as a main verb is put before the direct object that is given, here **tŭua** ตั๋ว *ticket*
- the indirect object to whom the object is given, here **rau** เรา, comes after

> **Short form**
> เขา ให้ ตั๋ว ไป เชียงใหม่
> kháu *hâi-tŭua* pai tʃiiang-mài
> he *give-ticket* go Chiang Mai

- the indirect object to whom the object is given, here **rau** เรา *we*, can be omitted if it is understood from the context

B. Understanding hâi ให้ and giving something to someone

- **hâi** ให้ *to give*
- **hâi** ให้ as a main verb

The most simple way to use the verb **hâi** ให้ is to use it as *to give something to someone*. Here **hâi** ให้ is used as a main verb without the help of any other verb.

Word order

hâi ให้ *to give* as a main verb is always put before the direct object that is given, and the indirect object to whom the object is given comes after.

> Subject + *hâi-ngən-tʃán*
> mother + *give-money-I* = mother gave me money

The direct object is here the noun *money*, and the indirect object is a pronoun *I*.

Example:

> Mother gave me money.
> แม่ ให้ เงิน ฉัน
> mɛ̂ɛ *hâi-ngən-tʃán*
> mother *give-money-I*

In Thai the direct object comes first after the action verb. In English the indirect object usually comes first.

- **hâi** ให้ *to give* as a main verb is put before the *direct object* that is given, **ngən** เงิน *money*
- *the indirect object*, to whom the money was given, comes after, here **tʃán** ฉัน *me*
- in English the structure is usually subject + indirect object + direct object = *Mother gave me money*
- we may use the similar structure to Thai in English, but then we need to insert the preposition *to* before the indirect object

subject + direct object + to + indirect object

= *Mother gave money to me.*

- however in Thai we don't really have a choice

Warning

It is not correct to say:

> Mother gave me money.
> แม่ ให้ ฉัน เงิน
> mɛ̂ɛ *hâi-tʃán-ngən*
> mother *give-I-money*

Note: Giving changes to letting

> Mother let me go to school.
> แม่ ให้ ฉัน ไป โรง เรียน
> mɛ̂ɛ *hâi-tʃán* pai roong-riian
> mother *let-I* go school

- when **hâi** ให้ is placed before the pronoun, **tʃán** ฉัน *I*, the meaning of **hâi** ให้ changes *to let*
- see more about **hâi** ให้ used as *letting, allowing, permitting* in Secret 4

Conclusion

We may conclude that **hâi** ให้ *to give*, used as a main verb, must be placed before the direct object, that is given, here **ngən** เงิน *money*.

The indirect object, who receives the money, here **tʃán** ฉัน *I,* follows directly after.

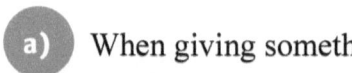

C. Language hints

When giving something to someone just place **hâi** ให้ to give before a direct object, a noun that is given. Examples of common nouns are money, cars, telephones, flowers etc... The indirect object, to whom the object is given, comes after.

a) When giving something

> Thais like to be intuitive, and in spoken Thai when the meaning is understood from the context, there is no need to say every word.

Secret 1 – hâi ให้ *to give* as a main verb

Example:

> Mother gave me money.
> แม่ ให้ เงิน ฉัน
> mɛ̂ɛ *hâi-ngən-tʃán*
> mother *give-money-I*

- the above statement may be shortened as follows:

> แม่ ให้
> mɛ̂ɛ *hâi*
> mother *give*

- you often hear that Thai people would only say **mɛ̂ɛ hâi** แม่ ให้
- these kinds of short expressions are commonly used when replying to a question like: "Who gave you money?"
- here both *direct* and *indirect objects* are dropped
- the whole meaning is understood from the context
- however, when the meaning cannot be understood from the context, the complete sentence is preferred

b) Note: Giving changes to letting

> They let us to go to Chiang Mai.
> พวก เขา ให้ เรา ไป เชียงใหม่
> phûuak-kháu *hâi-rau* pai tʃiiang-mài
> group-he *let-we* go Chiang Mai

- the meaning of **hâi** ให้ is here *to let*
- here **hâi** ให้ is placed before the pronoun, **rau** เรา *we*
- the meaning changes from *giving* to *letting*

- see also more about when **hâi** ให้ is used as *letting, allowing, permitting* in Secret 4

D. Simple advice

Note that when we translate sentences into English in this book, we give two different translations. First, the correct English translation of the overall sense of the meaning conveyed by the Thai phrase or sentence. Then the basic form, a literal word for word translation. Using this method you are hopefully able to follow the structure of the Thai language better. It may also help you to learn new words more easily.

The Thai language may seem to be very easy to learn because every word is in its basic form. For example: Verbs are not conjugated, there are no tenses for verbs, there are no plural forms for nouns and no genders or articles like a, an or the. As an illustration of this, in English we would say, "I drove him to the school", but the same in Thai would be, "I drive he school". The context would reveal the tense.

As you will learn in this book, because everything in Thai is in basic form, word order is often critical to meaning, much more so than in English. Thai may not therefore be as easy as it seems on the surface.

Secret 2 – hâi ให้ *to give* with kàp กับ and kὲε แก่

To give...to you
ให้...กับ คุณ
hâi...kàp khun

hâi meets with "kàp" and "kὲε" hâi says: "Hello "kàp" and "kὲε". I would like to be your friend."

ให้ เจอ กับ และ แก่ – ให้ บอก ว่า – สวัสดี ค่ะ กับ และ แก่ – ฉัน อยาก เป็น เพื่อน กับ พวก คุณ

hâi tɕɤɤ kàp lέ kὲε – hâi bɔ̀ɔk-wâa – sàwàtdii khâ kàp lέ kὲε – tʃǎn yàak pen phŵan kàp phûuak-khun

hâi meet "with" and "to" – hâi tell that – hello "with" and "to" – I want be friend with group-you

SECRET 2

hâi ให้ *to give* with **kàp** กับ and **kèɛ** แก่

hâi ให้ *to give* can be used with the words **kàp** กับ or **kèɛ** แก่ to make a statement more clear and profound.

Secret 2 – hâi ให้ *to give* with kàp กับ and kèɛ แก่

A. Sentences

To give with kàp กับ and kèɛ แก่

> **1**
> To give a book – hâi nǎng-sǔu ให้ หนังสือ
> I give this book to you.
> ฉัน ให้ หนังสือ เล่ม นี้ กับ คุณ
> tʃán hâi nǎng-sǔu lêm níi *kàp-khun*
> I give book copy this *with-you*

- **kàp khun** กับ คุณ *to you*

- here the longer statement using **kàp** กับ *with* is preferred since the direct object, that is given, *is separated from* the indirect object, here **khun** คุณ *you*

- the direct object **nǎng-sǔu** หนังสือ *book* is qualified by a classifier **lêm níi** เล่ม นี้ *this copy*

- in this context the word **kàp** กับ *with* is better translated into English as *to*

> **Short form**
> ฉัน ให้ เล่ม นี้ คุณ
> tʃán hâi lêm níi *khun*
> I give copy this *you*

- if the context is clear, the main word **nǎng-sǔu** หนังสือ *book* can be omitted

- a classifier **lêm níi** เล่ม นี้ *this copy* may be used alone

- also the word **kàp** กับ *with*, can be dropped if the context is clear

Secret 2 – hâi ให้ *to give* with kàp กับ and kèɛ แก่

> **To give a watch** – hâi naalikaa ให้ นาฬิกา
> I will give this watch to you soon.
> ฉัน จะ ให้ นาฬิกา เรือน นี้ แก่ คุณ อีก ไม่ นาน
> tʃán tsà hâi naalikaa-ruuan-níi *kèɛ-khun* iik-mâi-naan
> I will give watch-clock-this *to-you* more-no-long

- **kèɛ khun** แก่ คุณ *to you*
- **hâi** ให้ *to give* as a main verb is put before the direct object that is given, here **naalikaa-ruuan-níi** นาฬิกา เรือน นี้ *this watch*
- **kèɛ** แก่ *to* is placed before the indirect object, to whom the object is given, here **khun** คุณ *you*
- **kèɛ** แก่ is usually translated into English as *to* or *for*

> **Short form**
> จะ ให้ คุณ อีก ไม่ นาน
> tsà hâi *khun* iik-mâi-naan
> I will give *you* more-no-long

- when the context is clear the subject, **tʃán** ฉัน *I*, can be omitted
- also the direct object, **naalikaa-ruuan-níi** นาฬิกา เรือน นี้ *watch*, can be omitted
- then also the word **kèɛ** แก่ can be dropped
- **naalikaa-ruuan-níi** นาฬิกา เรือน นี้ *watch* remains a direct object, which is understood intuitively
- **khun** คุณ *you* is an indirect object, and the meaning of **hâi** ให้ is *to give*

Secret 2 – hâi ให้ *to give* with kàp กับ and kὲɛ แก่

3 To give experience – hâi pràsòpgaan ให้ ประสบการณ์

I gave him a good time.

ฉัน ให้ ประสบการณ์ ที่ ดี กับ เขา
tɕǎn hâi pràsòpgaan thîi dii *kàp-kháu*
I give experience that good *with-he*

- **kàp kháu** *to him*

- here the longer statement using **kàp** กับ *with* is preferred since the direct object, that is given, *is separated from* the indirect object, here **kháu** เขา *him*

- the direct object **pràsòpgaan** ประสบการณ์ *experience* is qualified by the words **thîi dii** ที่ ดี *that good*

- in this context the word **kàp** กับ *with* is better translated into English as *to*

Short form

ให้ ประสบการณ์ ที่ ดี กับ เขา
hâi pràsòpgaan thîi dii *kàp-kháu*
give experience that good *with-he*

- when the context is clear we can drop the subject **tɕǎn** ฉัน *I*

- it is not correct to drop **kàp** กับ *with*, because in practice the sentence would not be very clear. See more about this in the next section B

- there is **thîi dii** ที่ ดี *that good* between the direct object **pràsòpgaan** ประสบการณ์ *experience* and indirect object **kháu** เขา *him*

B. Understanding hâi with kàp กับ and kɛ̀ɛ แก่

- **hâi** ให้ *to give* with **kàp** กับ and **kɛ̀ɛ** แก่
- **hâi** ให้ *to give* as a main verb

In order to make a statement more clear, **hâi** ให้ can be used together with a number of other words. Here two words **kàp** กับ *with* and **kɛ̀ɛ** แก่ *for* are being used for greater clarity. They can be translated into English in this context as *to* or *for*.

Word order

hâi ให้ *to give* as a main verb is always put before the *direct object,* that what is given. **kàp** กับ or **kɛ̀ɛ** แก่ is put before the *indirect object,* to whom the object is given.

> Subject + hâi + năng-sŭɯ + *kàp-khun* or *kɛ̀ɛ-khun*
>
> I + give + book + *to-you* = I give a book to you

The direct object here is the noun *book,* and the indirect object is the pronoun *you.*

When the sentence is long, and when the *direct object,* that which is given, is separated from the *indirect object,* to whom the object is given, it is better to use **kàp** กับ or **kɛ̀ɛ** แก่ in order to avoid misunderstanding. See the sentences above.

These two words are interchangeable. The word **kàp** กับ is more informal and is used mainly when speaking. **kɛ̀ɛ** แก่ is more formal and can be used both when speaking and writing.

Usually, Thais like to make everything short, and there is no need to make a complete sentence in order to be correct as is often the case in English. However, when the sentence is long, and there is a possibility of misunderstanding, **kàp** กับ or **kɛ̀ɛ** แก่ are used to clarify the meaning.

In English this structure is similar to Thai I + give + this book + *to* + you = *I give this book to you.*

In English, however, we may also use the structure I + give + you + this book = *I give you this book.* See more about that in Secret 1.

> **Conclusion**
>
> We may conclude that **hâi** ให้ *to give*, used as a main verb, must be placed before the direct object that is given, here **năng-sŭu lêm níi** หนังสือ เล่ม นี้ *this book.*
>
> However, when the direct object is *qualified*, which means that there are words between the direct object and indirect object, then we need to place **kàp** กับ or **kèɛ** แก่ before the indirect object, the one who receives the book. *It is obligatory.* This gives the sentence greater clarity.

C. Language hints

Sometimes the situation calls for a complete and clear statement in order to avoid misunderstanding. On these occasions it is better to use the complete sentence with **kàp** กับ or **kèɛ** แก่.

Often when the sentence is constructed with the classifier, the longer term with **kàp** กับ or **kèɛ** แก่ is preferred. See section D. Simple advice and the definition of classifiers under grammar terms at the end of this book.

Using classifiers

Note that in the following sentence the word **lêm** เล่ม *copy, edition* is the classifier for the noun **năng-sŭu** หนังสือ *book*. The classifier is compulsory here since the word book is specified as *this book*. The classifier comes after the main word.

Secret 2 – hâi ให้ *to give* with kàp กับ and kɛ̀ɛ แก่

Example:

> I give this book to you.
> ฉัน ให้ หนังสือ เล่ม นี้ กับ คุณ
> tʃán hâi *năng-sŭu lêm-níi* kàp-khun
> I give *book copy-this* with-you

- **lêm** เล่ม *copy* is a classifier for the word **năng-sŭu** หนังสือ *book*
- here it is better to use also the word **kàp** กับ or **kɛ̀ɛ** แก่

> I give you this book.
> ฉัน ให้ เล่ม นี้ คุณ
> tʃán hâi *lêm-níi* khun
> I give *copy-this* you

- the word **năng-sŭu** หนังสือ *book* can be dropped, and only a classifier **lêm** เล่ม is used
- if the meaning is understood from the context and it is clear to which word the classifier **lêm** เล่ม is referring to, it is quite common in spoken Thai to drop the main word here **năng-sŭu** หนังสือ *book*
- in this case we may also drop the word **kàp** กับ
- note that some classifiers are used for several other words
- the word **lêm** เล่ม, for example, is used also as a classifier for **mîit** มีด *knives* and other sharp pointed objects like **thiian** เทียน *candles*
- if the context is not clear, the main word, here **năng-sŭu** หนังสือ *book,* can't be dropped

D. Simple advice

> Thai count nouns are called classifiers. Many Eastern languages such as Lao, Khmer, Chinese, Japanese, Vietnamise use classifiers as count nouns. English also uses classifiers with some words, for example: pair of shoes, head of cattle and bottles of milk. The difference is that in Thai it is always necessary to use classifiers. Therefore, you cannot say in Thai: "There are six students in the class", you need to say: "There is a student six persons in the class".

In the Khmer language, which has similar structure to Thai, classifiers are used much less, and it is not always necessary to use a classifier when speaking whilst in Thai it would be compulsory. If you are unable to use classifiers correctly in Thai you may be understood, but your language skills will be viewed by Thais as lacking something important.

> Note, however, that abstract nouns such as experience, price, authority etc., which cannot be touched, do not usually have any classifiers.

The whole usage of classifiers in Thai is somewhat contradictory to the Thai style of shortening phrases when speaking. Often it seems that a classifier does not contribute anything to understanding the meaning of the sentence. To the Western mind it is only a more complicated way to express the same meaning. However, no scholar in Thai language would agree with that. For Thai people classifiers have inherent meaning.

Speaking Thai is like a game. Learn the rules of the game and play it well. Do not be too serious! Keeping that in mind makes things easier and more relaxed.

Secret 3 – hâi ให้ changing nouns into verbs

To authorise
ให้ สิทธิ์
hâi-sìt

hâi meets "authority", "posture" and "forgiveness". These words want to become verbs. hâi says: "Do not worry. I can change you. Let me do it for you."

ให้ เจอ สิทธิ์ – ท่า และ อภัย – พวก เขา อยาก เป็น คำ กริยา – ให้ บอก ว่า – ไม่ ต้อง ห่วง ฉัน เปลี่ยน พวก คุณ ได้ – ให้ ฉัน ทำ ให้ นะ

hâi tsəə sìt – thâa lɛ́ àphai – phûuak-kháu yàak pen kham-grìyaa – hâi bɔ̀ɔk-wâa – mâi tôŋ hùuaŋ tʃán plìian phûuak-khun dâai – hâi tʃán tham-hâi ná

hâi meet authority – posture forgiveness and – group-he want be word-verb – hâi tell that – no need worry – I change group-you can – let I do-make ná

Secret 3

hâi ให้ changing nouns *into verbs*

hâi ให้ *to give* is often also used with a number of nouns to change them into a verb as far as the English language is concerned. These are usually abstract nouns, which cannot be touched. When the verb **hâi** ให้ *to give* is put before an abstract noun it sometimes changes a noun into a *verb*.

secret 3 – hâi ให้ changing nouns into verbs

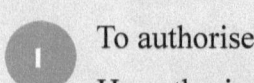

Making nouns become verbs

> **1**
>
> To authorise – hâi-sìt ให้ สิทธิ์
>
> He authorised me to use his red motorcycle for five days.
> เขา ให้ สิทธิ์ ฉัน ใช้ มอเตอร์ไซค์ คัน สี แดง ของ เขา ห้า วัน
> kháu *hâi-sìt-tʃán* tʃái mɔɔtəəsai khan sǐi dɛɛng khɔ̌ɔng kháu hâa wan
> he *give-authority-I* use motorcycle vehicle colour red of he five day

- **hâi-sìt** ให้ สิทธิ์ *to authorise*
- **hâi** ให้ *to give* is put before the direct object **sìt** สิทธิ์ *authority*
- in English the same is conveniently expressed by the verb *to authorise*
- **hâi-sìt** ให้ สิทธิ์ *to authorise* is somewhat formal and is not often used while speaking
- the pronoun **tʃán** ฉัน *me* is an indirect object here

> **Short form**
>
> เขา ให้ ใช้ คัน นี้ ห้า วัน
> kháu *hâi* tʃái khan-níi hâa wan
> he *give* use vehicle this five day

- the direct object **sìt** สิทธิ์ *authority* and the indirect object **tʃán** ฉัน *me* may be dropped
- the indirect object **tʃán** ฉัน *me* is understood intuitively from the context
- meaning of **hâi** ให้ becomes *to let* instead of *to authorise*
- see more about **hâi** ให้ *to let* in the next Secret 4

Secret 3 – hâi ให้ changing nouns into verbs

- also the word **mɔɔtəəsai** มอเตอร์ไซค์ *motorcycle* can be dropped
- it is quite common in spoken Thai that only a classifier **khan** คัน *vehicle* is used
- this will usually happen if it is understood from the context which word the classifier **khan** คัน vehicle is referring to

2

To flirt – hâi-thâa ให้ ท่า

Well-mannered girls don't flirt.

ผู้หญิง สุภาพ ๆ ไม่ ให้ ท่า
phûu yǐng sùphâap-sùphâap mâi *hâi-thâa*
person girl polite-polite no *give-posture*

- **hâi-thâa** ให้ ท่า *to flirt*
- **hâi** ให้ *to give* is put before the direct object **thâa** ท่า *a posture*
- in English the same is conveniently expressed by the verb *to flirt*
- this expression is not very appropriate in Thai since it carries a sexual connotation and is considered to be somewhat rude

Short form

ผู้หญิง สุภาพ ๆ ไม่ ให้ ท่า
phûu yǐng sùphâap-sùphâap mâi hâi-thâa
person girl polite-polite no give-postur

- the above sentence 2 can't really be made any shorter

3

To forgive – hâi-àphai ให้ อภัย

I have forgiven that person who did wrong to me.

ฉัน ให้ อภัย คน ที่ ทำ ผิด กับ ฉัน
tʃǎn *hâi-àphai-khon* thîi tham phìt kàp tʃǎn
I *give-forgiveness-person* that do wrong with I

Secret 3 – hâi ให้ changing nouns into verbs

- **hâi-àphai** ให้ อภัย *to forgive*
- **hâi** ให้ *to give* is put before the direct object **àphai** อภัย *forgiveness*
- in English the same is conveniently expressed by the verb *to forgive*

> **Short form**
> ฉัน ให้ อภัย
> tʃán *hâi-àphai*
> I *give-forgiveness*

- the second part of the sentence may be dropped provided it is understood from the context
- in Thai it is not necessary to speak out every word for the statement to be complete

B. Understanding hâi ให้ and making nouns become verbs

- **hâi** ให้ *to give* to make nouns become verbs
- **hâi** ให้ as a main verb

Word order
Put **hâi** ให้ as a main verb before an abstract noun to make it a verb.

> Subject + *hâi-sìt-tʃán*
>
> he + *give-authority-I* = he authorised me to...

Example:

> hâi-sìt ให้ สิทธิ์ *to authorise*

- **sìt** สิทธิ์ is an abstract noun with a Pali / Sanskrit origin meaning *authority, right*
- place **hâi** ให้ before the noun **sìt** สิทธิ์, and the translation into English is *to authorise*
- the exact translation into English would be *to give authority* or *right*
- **hâi** ให้ *to give* is usually used this way with some special abstract nouns only
- in cases like this the English language often seems to prefer *one word, a verb*

Conclusion

With some nouns **hâi** ให้ *to give* can be put before a noun to make it into a verb in English. These are usually abstract nouns. Abstract nouns are usually intangible, they cannot be touched.

As far as the Thai language is concerned, this structure is similar to that mentioned in Secret 1, where **hâi** ให้ is used as a main verb, and the direct object, that which is given, is placed directly after the verb **hâi** ให้ *to give*.

A similar structure is sometimes used in English in sentences like:

> He gave us an opportunity to try again.
> เขา ให้ โอกาส เรา ลองดู ใหม่
> kháu hâi ookàat rau lɔɔng-duu mài
> he give opportunity we try-see again.

Secret 3 – hâi ให้ changing nouns into verbs

> ### C. Language hints

> The Thai language contains a vast number of loan words which have been borrowed mainly from Khmer, Chinese and Indic languages such as Sanskrit and Pali. Recently, more words from English have been introduced into Thai.
>
> One notable point is that in Thai the original spelling of the loan word is often kept, but the pronunciation is modified to suit the way Thai is spoken. Hence many similar sounds are spelled differently from each other when written but pronounced the same.

khɔɔmphiutɤɤ คอมพิวเตอร์ *computer* is a loan word borrowed from English. **sìt** สิทธิ *authority* is a loan word borrowed from Indic languages. It is written with a rare consonant **t** ธ while **t** ท is a more common way to spell the same sound.

Note also that there are two written sounds at the end of the word **sìt** สิทธิ, which are not pronounced. These are the consonant sound **t** ธ and the vowel sound **ì** อิ. There is a killer symbol on the top to indicate that these sounds are not pronounced. Whenever you see the killer symbol you can assume that the word is borrowed either from English or from an Indic language.

More about classifiers:

> This computer.
> คอมพิวเตอร์ เครื่อง นี้
> khɔɔmphiutɤɤ *khrûang* níi
> computer *machine* this

- there must be a classifier **khrûang** เครื่อง *machine* since the word **khɔɔmphiutɤɤ** คอมพิวเตอร์ *computer* is specified by **níi** นี้ *this*
- **khrûang** เครื่อง *machine* is used as a classifier for computers, stereos, phones and other electrical and electronic appliances

> **Short form**
>
> This computer.
> เครื่อง นี้
> khrûang níi
> machine this

- in speaking a classifier alone may be used if the context is clear

D. Simple advice

It is worthwhile clarifying the difference in meaning between a *direct object* and an *indirect object* as introduced in Secrets 1–3. They are used somewhat differently in Thai and in English. In both languages the direct object is that which is given, and the indirect object is the receiver, the person who gets the object. However, the word order is usually different in Thai from the word order in English. See Secret 1.

> Grammar in Thai may seem to be very straightforward. However, you need to be sensitive to the context, quickly understand it and know to whom you are speaking. Thai people, as native speakers, will understand everything very fast, and probably be one step ahead of you in a conversation. The Thai people prefer short sentences and drop many words, which are understood from the context.

In the following Secrets we shall show that the meaning of **hâi** ให้ is often understood intuitively from the context. As a causative verb it carries several different meanings depending on the situation, and the way it is spoken. It can be translated into English as *to let, to allow, to make, to request* or *to order* someone to do something.

In some situations **hâi** ให้ is better translated into English as *for: for you, for me*. It is also often used in idiomatic phrases where it carries no meaning itself but only a sense of command.

PART II

hâi ให้ as a causative verb
for *letting, requesting, ordering*

I let
ฉัน ให้
tʃán hâi

hâi has many meanings. **hâi** says: "I can be very flexible. Sometimes I can also change the meaning of myself. I'll show you."

ให้ มี ความ หมาย หลวย อย่าง – ให้ บอก ว่า – ฉัน พลิก แพลง ได้ ง่าย – บาง ครัง ก็ เปลี่ยน ความ หมาย ตัว เอง ได้ – ฉัน จะ แสดง ให้ คุณ ดู

hâi mii khwaam-măai lăai yàang – **hâi** bɔ̀ɔk-wâa – tʃán phlík-phlɛɛng dâai ngâai – bâang khráng gɔ̂ɔ pliian khwaam-măai tuua-eng dâai – tʃán tsà sàdɛɛng hâi khun duu

hâi have matter-meaning many type – **hâi** tell that I flexible can easy – some time also change matter-aim body-self can – I will show let you see

Secret 4

hâi ให้ as a causative main verb for *letting, requesting, ordering*

When **hâi** ให้ is used as a causative verb, that means that we cause someone else to perform the task. The same simple statement with the word **hâi** ให้ *to let* in Thai has a range of meanings; from *pure letting* to *strict ordering* all depending on how it is said.

Secret 4 – hâi ให้ as a causative main verb

A. Sentences

hâi ให้ as a causative verb

> **1** Letting, allowing, permitting – hâi ให้
>
> I'll let you go to Phuket.
>
> ฉัน ให้ คุณ ไป ภูเก็ต
>
> tʃán *hâi-khun* pai phuukèt
>
> I *let-you* go Phuket

- **hâi** ให้ *to let, to allow, to permit*
- **hâi** ให้ *to let* as a causative verb is placed before the pronoun, here **khun** คุณ *you* followed by the action verb **pai** ไป *to go*
- the meaning *to let, to allow, to permit* is understood from the context, and how the statement is said
- English has several different words to express *to let* such as *to allow* or *to permit*

> **Short form**
>
> ฉัน ให้ คุณ ไป
>
> tʃán *hâi-khun* pai
>
> I *let-you* go

- when the context is clear, the word **Phuket** ภูเก็ต can be dropped

> **2** Wanting, demanding, requesting – hâi ให้
>
> He requested me to finish it.
>
> เขา ให้ ฉัน ทำ ให้ เสร็จ
>
> kháu *hâi-tʃán* tham hâi sèt
>
> he *request-I* do let finish

- **hâi** ให้ *to want, to demand, to request*

Secret 4 – hâi ให้ as a causative main verb

- **hâi** ให้ *to request* as a causative verb is placed before the pronoun, here **tʃán** ฉัน *I,* followed by the action verb, **tham** ทำ *to do*
- the meaning is understood from the context and how the statement is said
- this statement is somewhere between *to let* (sentence 1) and *to make* (sentence 3) someone do someting
- we may use here different English translations, which denote slightly different meanings, such as *He wanted me to finish it* or *He demanded that I should finish it*

Short form

เขา ให้ ทำ ให้ เสร็จ
kháu *hâi* tham hâi sèt
he *request* do make finish

- when the context is clear then the pronoun **tʃán** ฉัน *I* can be dropped in speaking

3 Ordering, making, forcing – hâi ให้

He ordered me to come here.

เขา ให้ ฉัน มา ที่ นี่
kháu *hâi-tʃán* maa thîi-nîi
he *make-I* come place this

- **hâi** ให้ *to order, to make, to force*
- **hâi** ให้ *to order* as a causative verb is placed before the pronoun **tʃán** ฉัน *I* followed by the action verb maa มา *to come*
- this sentence could also mean *to let* or *to request*
- the meaning of firm *ordering* is understood from the context, and how the statement is said
- English has several different words to express causative *ordering*, which denote slightly different meanings

- this sentence could also be translated as:

He made me come here.
He had me come here.
He got me to come here.
He forced me to come here.
He requested me to come here.
He let me come here.

> **Short form**
> เขา ให้ ฉัน มา
> kháu *hâi-tʃán* maa
> he *make-I* come

- when the context is clear then the word **thîi-nîi** ที่ นี่ *here* can be dropped

B. Understanding hâi ให้ as a causative verb

- **hâi** ให้ *to let, to allow, to request, to order*
- **hâi** ให้ as a causative verb alone

The verb **hâi** ให้ as a causative verb may have several meanings when translated to English.

Word order

For Thai people **hâi** ให้ is one word, and the meaning is *to give*. However, its semantic boundary is much wider than the usage of the English word *to give*. Therefore, we need to use several different English words to grasp the correct meaning of **hâi** ให้.

Put **hâi** ให้ before the pronoun to whom the action is directed followed by the action verb as follows:

Secret 4 – hâi ให้ as a causative main verb

> Subject + *hâi-khun* + Verb
>
>   I + *let-you* + go
>   I + *request-you* + go
>   I + *make-you* + go

As a causative verb **hâi** ให้ is usually placed before the pronoun.

The single verb **hâi** ให้ can play the role of many different causative English verbs. **hâi** ให้ denotes a different degree of action, namely; *to allow, to request, to make* or even *to order* or *to force* someone to do something depending upon the context, and how the statement is said.

> When **hâi** ให้ is used as a causative verb it means that the subject is *letting* or *making* someone else perform the task.

> The common causative verbs in English are *to let, to make, to get, to have*. In English common causative constructions are often expressed using the passive voice as in *I had my hair cut.*

In Thai the causative construction is usually expressed with the help of the verb **hâi** ให้.

Example:

> I'll let you go.
> ผม ให้ คุณ ไป
> phŏm *hâi-khun* pai
> I *let-you* go

- here **phŏm** ผม *I* is the subject, and the causative verb **hâi** ให้ is placed before the pronoun, **khun** คุณ *you*

The above simple Thai sentence may be translated into English in several different ways depending on the situation:

I allow you to go.
I want you to go.
I request you to go.
I make you go.
I order you to go.
I force you to go.
I had you go.
I got you to go.

- when **hâi** ให้ is used alone as a causative verb, we need to be aware of the context and how the statement is said
- when the tone or the voice level is changed, the meaning may be different

When you are reading, you need to understand the meaning from the context only or perhaps from an additional helping verb, which is used with **hâi** ให้ to make a statement clearer.

Some common verbs used together with **hâi** ให้ to make a statement clearer as follows:

- yɔɔm-**hâi** ยอม ให้ *to let, to allow, to permit, to surrender*
- yàak-**hâi** อยาก ให้ *to ask, to wish, to request*
- sàng-**hâi** สั่ง ให้ *strong ordering, forcing*

An additional verb together with **hâi** ให้ makes the statement clearer and stronger. There is a lower probability of misunderstanding. When writing, it is therefore often better to use the helping verb together with **hâi** ให้.

- see more about **hâi** ให้ *to let, to allow, to permit* used as a causative compound verb in Secret 5
- see more about **hâi** ให้ *to request, to want, to demand* as a causative compound verb in Secret 6
- see more about **hâi** ให้ *strong ordering* or *forcing* as a causative compound verb in Secret 7

Secret 4 – hâi ให้ as a causative main verb

However when speaking, hâi ให้ *to let, to request* or *to order* is usually used alone as a causative verb without another verb since comprehension is easier and intuitive. Thai people like that.

In Secrets 1–3 we may directly translate the meaning of **hâi** ให้ into English as *to give*.

> **Conclusion**
>
> We may conclude that when **hâi** ให้ is used as a causative verb, it is usually placed before a pronoun, someone who needs to carry out the action. As a causative verb **hâi** ให้ points out the person whom the action is directed to. The action verb, what type of action is in question, comes after.
>
> The single word **hâi** ให้ is used for seemingly different English meanings. It is however the same verb, and the difference in meaning is understood from the context and how the statement is said.
>
> In this Secret, when **hâi** ให้ is used as a causative verb, we need to expand its semantic boundaries to include the English verbs *to let* and *to request* or even *to have, to make* or *to order* someone do something.
>
> The beauty of this kind of construction is, that it gives the listener, in the given context, the chance of having her own free, personal and flexible interpretation of the verb **hâi** ให้.

C. Language hints

In Thai words tend to lose their meaning if there is no feeling involved.

Note that we have transliterated in this Secret **hâi** ให้ literally as *to let, to request* and *to order*. However, it denotes many different meanings and words in English.

For Thai people **hâi** ให้ is one word, and they don't usually give it different meanings. They understand the meaning intuitively from the context.

Consider the following sentences:

Examples:

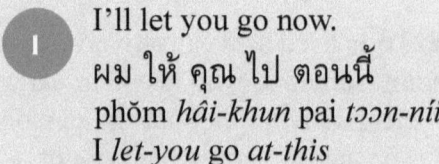

> I'll let you go now.
> ผม ให้ คุณ ไป ตอนนี้
> phŏm *hâi-khun* pai *tɔɔn-níi*
> I *let-you* go *at-this*

- in this sentence, **hâi** ให้ could be translated into English in three basic ways:

> I'll *let* you go now.
> I *request* you go now.
> I *order* you to go now.

- here **hâi** ให้ is used as a causative verb, and it is placed before a direct object, which is a pronoun, here **khun** คุณ *you*

- depending upon how the statement is said, it has clearly different semantic meanings in English

- when **hâi** ให้ is used alone for *ordering*, the statement can be emphasised with the particles like **tɔɔn-níi** ตอนนี้ *right now* or **than-thii** ทันที *immediately*

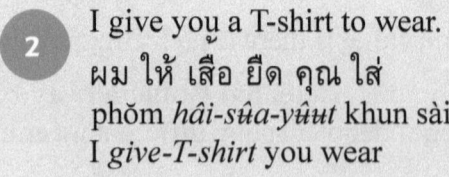

> I give you a T-shirt to wear.
> ผม ให้ เสื้อ ยืด คุณ ใส่
> phŏm *hâi-sûa-yûut* khun sài
> I *give-T-shirt* you wear

Secret 4 – hâi ให้ as a causative main verb

- here **hâi** ให้ means *to give* since it is put before the direct object, which is a noun **sûa-yûut** เสื้อ ยืด *T-shirt*
- the pronoun, **khun** คุณ *you* becomes here an indirect object
- see more about this type of structure in Secret 1

> **3** I let you wear T-shirt.
> ผม ให้ คุณ ใส่ เสื้อ ยืด
> phŏm *hâi-khun* sài sûa-yûut
> I *let-you* wear T-shirt

- here **hâi** ให้ is used as a causative verb, and it is placed before a direct object, which is a pronoun, here **khun** คุณ *you*
- in this sentence **hâi** ให้ means *to let*
- *letting, allowing, permitting* is understood from the context
- it is unlikely that you are forcing someone to use the T-shirt

D. Simple advice

The correct meaning of **hâi** ให้, as a causative verb, is understood very intuitively from the way the statement is said and from the context.

> When **hâi** ให้ is used as a causative verb, that means that we cause someone else to perform the task. We usually take the responsibility but someone else needs to carry out the action. Common causative verbs in English are *to let, to have* and *to make*.

Thai people like to interact with each other. When you interact with people you need to be engaged with them. That cannot be done without feelings and empathy. These feelings are strongly related to meaning and comprehension in Thai.

> If you just put words together one after another in a monotonous voice without any feeling, you can almost be sure that you will not be understood by Thais. Many other languages like German and even English can be spoken like that without losing the meaning, but not Thai.

Secret 5 – hâi ให้ for *making something happen*

To make, to cause
ทำ ให้
Tham-hâi

> hâi has a very good heart, and she is also fun. hâi says: "I like to feel happy. I do not want to make anybody feel bad."
>
> ให้ เป็น คน ที่ ใจ ดี จัง และ สนุก ด้วย – ให้ บอก ว่า – ฉัน อยาก มี ความ สุข – ไม่ อยาก ทำ ให้ ใคร รู้ สึก แย่
>
> hâi pen khon thîi tsai-dii tsang lɛ́ sànùk dûuai – hâi bɔ̀ɔk-wâa – tʃán yàak mii khwaam-sùk – mâi yàak tham-hâi khrai rúu-sùk yɛ̂ɛ
>
> hâi is person that heart-good very and fun also – hâi tell that – I want have matter-happy – no want do-make who know-awareness terrible

SECRET 5

hâi ให้ as a causative compound verb for *making something happen*

To make something happen or a condition to change, Thai uses a causative verb construction **tham-hâi** ทำ ให้. It is used frequently in daily conversation in Thai.

Other compound verbs may be used depending on the context such as **tʃûuai-hâi**... ช่วย ให้ *to help something to happen*.

A. Sentences

hâi ให้ as a causative compound verb for making something happen

1 To make... – tham-hâi ทำ ให้...

You make me feel happy.

คุณ ทำ ให้ ฉัน รู้ สึก มี ความ สุข
khun *tham-hâi-tʃán* rúu-sùk mii khwaam-sùk
you *do-make-I* know-awareness have matter-happy

- **tham-hâi** ทำ ให้ *to make*
- **hâi** ให้ can be used together with the verb **tham** ทำ *to do, to make* or *to cause* the condition to change, here *to feel happy*
- before he was not so happy. Now he is happy! The condition has changed

Short form

คุณ ทำ ให้ ฉัน มี ความ สุข
khun *tham-hâi-tʃán* mii khwaam-sùk
you *do-make-I* have matter-happy

- the verb **rúu-sùk** รู้ สึก *to feel* can be dropped here without changing the meaning

2 Do not make... – yàa tham-hâi... อย่า ทำ ให้

Speak, think and do only good things, and don't make anybody feel tense.

พูด ดี คิด ดี ทำ ดี – อย่า ทำ ให้ ใคร เครียด
phûut dii khít dii tham dii – yàa *tham-hâi-khrai* khrîiat
speak good think good do good – no *do-make-who* tense

- **yàa tham-hâi...** อย่า ทำ ให้ *do not make*

Secret 5 – hâi ให้ for *making something happen*

- **hâi** ให้ is used together with the verb **yàa tham** อย่า ทำ *don't make*

- this sentence is a kind of negative command *or* warning – not to make the condition change, here, *not make anybody feel tense*

> **Short form**
>
> พูด ดี คิด ดี ทำ ดี – อย่า ให้ ใคร เครียด
> phûut dii khít dii tham dii yàa – *hâi-khrai* khrîiat
> speak good think good do good – no *make-who* tense

- the verb combination **tham-hâi** ทำ ให้ *to make* can be shortened to the verb **hâi** only

- using the verb **hâi** ให้ alone does not change much the meaning here

- the colour of the statement is a little different, however

> **3** To help... – tʃûuai-hâi... ช่วย ให้...
>
> He helped my dream come true.
>
> เขา ช่วย ให้ ความ ฝัน ของ ฉัน เป็น จริง
> kháu *tʃûuai-hâi-khwaam-fǎn* kɔ̌ɔng tʃǎn pen tsing
> he *help-make-matter-dream* of I be true

- **tʃûuai-hâi**...ช่วย ให้...*to help*

- **hâi** ให้ is used together with the verb **tʃûuai** ช่วย *to help*

- he *was helped* to achieve his dream

> **Short form**
>
> เขา ช่วย ให้ ความ ฝัน ฉัน เป็น จริง
> kháu *tʃûuai-hâi khwaam-fǎn* tʃǎn pen tsing
> he *help-make-matter-dream* I be true

- the possessive form **kɔ̌ɔng** ของ *of* can be dropped here without changing the meaning
- in spoken Thai the short version of the possessive form is usually preferred

> **B. Understanding hâi ให้ as a causative compound verb for making something happen**

- **hâi** ให้ as a causative compound verb for *making* or *causing* something to happen
- **hâi** ให้ as a second element in the compound verb

hâi ให้ is often used together with the verb **tham** ทำ *to do* to make or cause a condition to change, to make something happen.

When we use the term *compound verb* in Thai, we mean that there is a close connection between **hâi** ให้ and the other verb. They are not usually separated.

Word order

Put **tham-hâi** ทำ ให้ *to make* before the object to whom the action is directed as follows:

> Subject + *tham-hâi-tʃǎn* + verb
>
> he + *do-make-I* + go = he made me to go

Example:

> He made me tired.
> เขา ทำ ให้ ฉัน เหนื่อย
> kháu *tham-hâi-tʃǎn* nùuai
> he *do-make-I* tired

- **tham-hâi** ทำ ให้ *to make* is frequently used in Thai to express the cause that makes the condition change

> **Conclusion**
>
> We may conclude that when **hâi** ให้ is used as a causative compound verb, it is usually placed before a pronoun, someone who needs to carry out the action. As a causative compound verb **hâi** ให้ points out the person to whom the action is directed.
>
> In this Secret, when **hâi** ให้ is used as a causative compound verb, its semantic boundaries are also defined by the other verb that is used with it.
>
> For Thai people **hâi** ให้ is one word, and the meaning is *to give*. However, its semantic boundary is much wider than the usage of the English word *to give*. Therefore, we need to use several different English words to grasp the correct meaning of **hâi** ให้. See more about the term "semantic boundary" and other grammar terms at the end of this book.
>
> The other verb together with **hâi** ให้ clarifies the meaning, such as **tham-hâi** ทำ ให้ *to cause* or *to make*. The action verb, what type of action is in question, comes later in the sentence. The word order is Subject + *tham-hâi-tʃán* + verb

C. Language hints

In order to speak Thai well you need to understand how the prefixes are used in Thai.

In Thai there are several prefixes, which are used either before verbs or adjectives to change the meaning.

Two very common prefixes before verbs or adjectives are:

1 Converting verbs into nouns:

khwaam	ความ	prefix
khwaam-rúu	ความรู้	*knowledge*
khwaam-khít	ความคิด	*idea, thought*
khwaam-făn	ความ ฝัน	*dream*

- note that **khwaam-făn** ความ ฝัน a dream consists of two words **khwaam** ความ matter (prefix) and **făn** ฝัน to dream
- the prefix **khwaam** ความ converts verbs into abstract nouns

2 **gaan** การ prefix

gaan-hâi	การให้	*giving*
gaan-dâai	การได้	*getting*
gaan-mii	การมี	*having*

- **gaan** การ is another prefix, which is usually used only with verbs to convert them into a noun
- this kind on construction is called a "gerund" in English

3 Converting adjectives into nouns:

khwaam-nùuai	ความ เหนื่อย	*tiredness*
khwaam-sŭuai	ความ สวย	*beauty*
khwaam-sŭung	ความ สูง	*height*

- the prefix **khwaam** ความ converts adjectives into an abstract noun

There are many more prefixes commonly used in Thai, but to explain them here is beyond the scope of this book. We give here a few more examples:

tsâu เจ้า *skilful person*

Playboy

คน เจ้า ชู้
tsâu-tʃúu
person-lover

---

khâa ค่า *fee*

Renting fee

ค่า เช่า
khâa-tʃâu
fee-rent

---

kham คำ *word*

Translation

คำ แปล
kham-plɛɛ
word-translate

---

khɔ̂ɔ ข้อ *item*

Information

ข้อ มูล
khɔ̂ɔ-muun
item-information

> **khîi** ขี้ *prefix with negative connotation*
>
> *Lazy person*
>
> ขี้ เกียจ
> khîi-kìiat
> person-lazy

> **nâa** น่า *worthy of...*
>
> *Attractive*
>
> น่า ดู
> nâa-duu
> worthy-see

D. Simple advice

> Be more concerned with *how* rather than *why*. For Thai people, language is about communication and having fun rather than a complicated theory to be understood.

If your sentence is not correct Thai, and you would like to know what is the proper way to say it, you will often find Thai people say "You are right, but we do not say it like that".

> Often there is no why! Yet, having said that, try to understand how Thai people put words together in a sentence.

Perhaps you feel relieved to know that Thai people themselves do not always use the correct tone in every situation. The context in which you use a word is very important. If you use the correct word in the right situation and pronounce it correctly, Thai people will most likely understand you even if the tone is not quite right.

Won't *let*...
ยอม ให้...
mâi yɔɔm-hâi...

hâi likes freedom and wants everybody to be independent. hâi says: "When we allow children to study those subjects that they like, they become responsible people."

ให้ ชอบ เสรี และ คิด ว่า เรา ต้อง ให้ อิสระ กับ ทุกคน – ให้ บอก ว่า – เมื่อ เรา ยอม ให้ เด็กๆ เรียน วิชา ที่ เขา ชอบ – เขา จะ เป็น คน ที่ มี ความ รับผิดชอบ ได้

hâi tʃɔ̂ɔp sěerii lɛ́ khít wâa rau tôŋ hâi ìtsàrà kàp thúk-khon – hâi bɔ̀ɔk-wâa – mûɯa rau yɔɔm-hâi dèk-dèk riian wíttʃaa thîi kháu tʃɔ̂ɔp kháu tsà pen khon thîi mii kwaam-ráp-phìt-tʃɔ̂ɔp dâai

hâi like freedom and think that we must give independent with every-person – hâi tell that – when we allow-let child-child study subject that he like he will be person that have matter-receive-wrong-correct can

SECRET 6

hâi ให้ as a causative compound verb for *letting, allowing, permitting*

The compound verb *to let, to allow, to permit* something to happen in Thai is **yɔɔm-hâi** ยอม ให้. Other compound verbs like **ànúyâat-hâi** อนุญาต ให้ *to allow*, **plɔ̀ɔi-hâi** ปล่อย ให้ *to release* are used depending on the situation.

The compound verb with **hâi** ให้ *to let, to allow* cannot be as easily misunderstood unlike when the verb **hâi** ให้ is used alone for *letting*. In this structure the verb **hâi** ให้ is placed directly after the other verb.

A. Sentences

hâi ให้ as a causative compound verb for *allowing*

> **I** Letting, allowing, permitting – yɔɔm-hâi ยอม ให้
>
> I won't let you win.
> ฉัน ไม่ ยอม ให้ คุณ ชนะ
> tʃán mâi *yɔɔm-hâi-khun* tʃáná
> I no *allow-let-you* win

- **yɔɔm-hâi** ยอม ให้ *to let, to allow, to permit, to give up*
- **hâi** ให้ *to let* can be used together with the verb **yɔɔm** ยอม *to give in, to give up, to surrender* in order to make the meaning clear
- **yɔɔm-hâi** ยอม ให้ *to allow* is placed before the pronoun, here **khun** คุณ *you*
- the action verb, here **tʃáná** ชนะ *to win,* comes after
- **yɔɔm-hâi** ยอม ให้ is often used in speaking and in informal situations in the negative sentence
- **yɔɔm-hâi** ยอม ให้ can also be translated into English as *to let* and *to give up*

> **Short form**
> ฉัน ไม่ ให้ คุณ ชนะ
> tʃán mâi *hâi-khun* tʃáná
> I no *let-you* win

- in spoken Thai the other verb, here **yɔɔm** ยอม *to surrender*, is often dropped
- the meaning is nearly the same as in the complete sentence
- only the colour of the statement is different

- however, all depends on the context, and how the statement is said

> **2** Another word for letting, allowing, permitting
> – ànúyâat-hâi อนุญาต ให้
>
> He permitted me to go on the trip.
> เขา อนุญาต ให้ ฉัน ไป เที่ยว
> kháu *ànúyâat-hâi-tʃán* pai thîiau
> he *permit-let-I* go trip

- **ànúyâat-hâi** อนุญาต ให้ *to permit, to allow*
- **ànúyâat-hâi** อนุญาต ให้ *to allow* is more formal than **yɔɔm-hâi** ยอม ให้ *to allow*
- it is more often used in writing and when speaking in formal situations and when someone has the authority to give a permission

Short form
> เขา ให้ ไป
> kháu *hâi* pai
> he *let* go

- when replying to a question, and when the meaning is understood from the context, Thais like to use the short form like this
- in spoken Thai **hâi** ให้ is often used alone instead of the compound **ànúyâat-hâi** อนุญาต ให้ *to permit, to allow*
- also the object may be dropped, here **tʃán** ฉัน *me*
- the meaning is nearly the same as in the complete sentence. Only the colour of the statement is different
- however, everything depends on the context, and how the short form statement is said
- this short form is more casual than the complete sentence with **ànúyâat-hâi** อนุญาต ให้ *to permit / to allow*

> **3** Releasing, allowing, permitting – plɔ̀ɔi-hâi ปล่อย ให้
>
> I won't let you go.
> ฉัน จะ ปล่อย ให้ คุณ ไป ไม่ ได้
> tʃán tsà *plɔ̀ɔy-hâi-khun* pai mâi-dâai
> I will *release-let-you* go no able

- **plɔ̀ɔi-hâi** ปล่อย ให้ *to release, to allow, to permit*
- **plɔ̀ɔi-hâi** ปล่อย ให้ *to release* is another way of expressing *letting, permitting* compared to **yɔɔm-hâi** ยอม ให้ *to allow* or **ànúyâat-hâi** อนุญาต ให้ *to permit*

> **Short form**
> จะ ให้ คุณ ไป ไม่ ได้
> tsà *hâi-khun* pai mâi-dâai
> I will *let-you* go no-able

- when speaking, another verb, here **plɔ̀ɔi** ปล่อย *to release*, can be dropped without changing the meaning much

B. Understanding hâi ให้ as a causative

- **hâi** ให้ as a compound verb *to let, to allow, to permit*
- **hâi** ให้ as a second element in the compound verb

As a causative compound verb **hâi** ให้ is usually placed after the other verb.

When we use the term *compound verb*, we mean that there is a close connection between **hâi** ให้ and the other verb. They are not usually separated.

hâi ให้ in a compound structure with another verb forms one meaning.

Word order

Put **hâi** ให้ after another verb and before the object to whom the action is directed, followed by an additional action verb as follows:

> Subject + *yɔɔm-hâi-khun* + verb
>
> I + *allow-let-you* + win = I let you win (I give up)

In the previous Secret **hâi** ให้ was used as a causative verb alone. Often the situation calls for a clearer statement, or one wants to express nuances or a particular feeling with words. In these cases an additional verb is put before **hâi** ให้.

This structure is usually quite "tight" in the sense that **hâi** ให้ is attached to the other verb in such a way that it is not possible to put another word between the two.

> There are some other ways to express *letting, allowing, permitting*. Each way carries a somewhat different feeling, which is not always easy to translate exactly into English.
>
> We introduce here three compound verbs for *to let, to allow* and *to permit*.

- **yɔɔm-hâi** ยอม ให้ *to allow* is used mainly in speaking and in informal situations. It is often used in a negative sense. **yɔɔm-hâi** ยอม ให้ *to allow* can also be translated into English as *to let* or *to give up*

- **ànúyâat-hâi** อนุญาต ให้ *to allow* is more formal than **yɔɔm-hâi** ยอม ให้. It is often used in written language and formal situations. **ànúyâat-hâi** อนุญาต ให้ *to allow* can also be translated into English as *to permit*

- **plɔ̀ɔi-hâi** ปล่อย ให้ *to release* can also be translated as *to let, to allow* depending on the context and how it is said

- **hâi** ให้ together with the other verb makes a statement strong and clear

Using **hâi** ให้ alone is also translated as *to let, to allow* or *to permit*. Note, however, that it depends on how the statement is said. In some cases it can be translated into English as *to request* and even *to order*. This is the beauty of the Thai language, which allows you to express shades of meaning with feelings and with the tone of your voice.

hâi ให้ alone without another verb is mainly used in speaking. See more about that in Secret 4.

> **Conclusion**
>
> We may conclude that when **hâi** ให้ is used as a *causative compound verb*, it is usually placed before a pronoun, someone who needs to carry out the action. As a causative verb **hâi** ให้ points out the person whom the action is directed to.
>
> In this Secret, when **hâi** ให้ is used as a causative compound verb, its semantic boundaries are also defined by the additional verb that it is used with.
>
> For Thai people **hâi** ให้ is one word, and the meaning is *to give*. However, its semantic boundary is much wider than the usage of the English word *to give*. Therefore, we need to use several different English words to grasp the correct meaning of **hâi** ให้. See more about the term "semantic boundary" and other grammar terms at the end of this book.

> The additional verb used with **hâi** ให้ clarifies the meaning, such as **yɔɔm-hâi** ยอม ให้ *to let, to allow, to permit, to give up*. The action verb, what type of action is in question, comes after.

C. Language hints

When expressing *letting, allowing, permitting* with compound verbs such as **yɔɔm-hâi** ยอม ให้, *to allow, to give up*, **ànúyâat-hâi** อนุญาต ให้ *to allow* and **plɔ̀ɔi-hâi** ปล่อย ให้ *to release*, it depends on the person and the situation which verb is used.

Secret 6 – hâi ให้ for *allowing*

Using the above verbs without **hâi** ให้ is not always possible because it can change the meaning.

Grammatically, these three verbs behave differently when used alone.

Examples:

> **1**
> He doesn't give up.
> เขา ไม่ยอม
> kháu mâi *yɔɔm*
> he no *give up*

- **yɔɔm** ยอม can be used alone but the meaning is simply *to give up, to surrender*

> **2**   **Warning**
> It is not correct to say:
> He allowed me to go on the trip.
> เขา อนุญาต ฉัน ไป เที่ยว
> kháu *ànúyâat* tʃán pai thîiau
> he *allow* I go trip

- here the verb **ànúyâat** อนุญาต *to allow* can't be used alone without the verb **hâi** ให้ *to let*

- it doesn't sound right to native speakers. The correct sentence in Thai is kháu *ànúyâat* **hâi** tʃán pai thîiau เขา อนุญาต ให้ ฉัน ไป เที่ยว

> **2.1**
> Yes, he allowed.
> อนุญาต
> *ànúyâat*
> allow

- in short one word replies **ànúyâat** อนุญาต *to allow, to permit* can be used alone

> **3** I won't let you go. (in the sense of I can't let you go)
> จะ ปล่อย คุณ ไป ไม่ ได้
> tsà *plɔ̀ɔi-khun* pai mâi-dâai
> will *release-you* no-can

- here we have dropped **hâi** ให้, and the other verb **plɔ̀ɔi** ปล่อย *to release* is used alone
- the emphasis is here on the verb **plɔ̀ɔi** ปล่อย *to release*
- **plɔ̀ɔi** ปล่อย *to release* can be used alone in the sentence

> **3.1** จะ ให้ คุณ ไป ไม่ ได้
> tsà *hâi-khun* pai mâi-dâai
> I will *let-you* go no-can

- in this sentence we use **hâi** ให้ alone without the other verb
- this sentence could be translated into English the same as sentence 3. Only the colour of the statement is different
- here the emphasis is on the verb **hâi** ให้ *to let, to allow*

> **3.2** ฉัน จะ ปล่อย ให้ คุณ ไป ไม่ ได้
> tʃán tsà *plɔ̀ɔy-hâi-khun* pai mâi-dâai
> I will *release-let-you* go no able

- **plɔ̀ɔi-hâi** ปล่อย ให้ *to release, to allow, to permit*
- in this sentence we use **hâi** ให้ and **plɔ̀ɔi** ปล่อย together
- this sentence could be translated into English roughly the same as the above two sentences 3 and 3.1. Only the colour of the statement is different
- here the emphasis is on the verbs **hâi** ให้ *to let, to allow* and **plɔ̀ɔi** ปล่อย *to release*

D. Simple advice

Before you are able intuitively to use **hâi** ให้ correctly as Thai people do, you may need to understand the grammatical structure of the different ways it is used. The time you invest in learning the correct structure of the Thai language, as shown in this book, will pay off later. You will be able to make grammatically correct sentences as Thai people do.

You may have already noted that understanding the grammar rules as such is not very important for Thais. Sometimes, even Thai teachers are not able to give you the type of satisfactory grammatical explanations that we are used to with western languages. However, they know what is correct and what is wrong since they are born into the habit of speaking Thai correctly.

To ask
ขอ ให้
khɔ̌ɔ-hâi

hâi is a person, who understands the Thai language very well. **hâi** says: "This group of four different words for wanting, which are similar in usage, should be clearly understood."

ให้ เป็น คน ที่ เข้า ใจ ภาษา ไทย ดี มาก – ให้ บอก ว่า – คำ เหล่า นี้ "อยาก ให้" "อยาก ได้" "ต้อง การ ให้" "เอา" มี ความ หมาย คล้ายๆ กัน – คำ เหล่า นี้ เรา ต้อง เข้า ใจ ให้ ดี

hâi pen khon thîi khâu-tsai phaasǎa-thai dii mâak – **hâi** bɔ̀ɔk-wâa – kham làu níi *yàak-hâi yàak-dâai tôŋ-gaan-hâi au* mii khwaam-mǎai khláai-khláai kan – kham làu níi rau tôŋ khâu-tsai hâi dii

hâi be person that enter-heart language thai good very – **hâi** tell that – word group this *want-make want-get require-make want* have matter-aim similar-similar with – word group this we must enter-heart make good

Secret 7

hâi ให้ as a causative compound verb for *asking, wanting, requesting*

Wanting and *requesting* is usually expressed with the pattern **yàak-hâi** อยาก ให้ *to want* or **tông-gaan hâi** ต้อง การ ให้ *to request*.

Other compound verbs like **khɔ̌ɔ-hâi** ขอ ให้ *to ask* or **bɔ̀ɔk-hâi** บอก ให้ *to tell* may be used depending on the situation.

Secret 7 – hâi ให้ for *making a request*

A. Sentences

hâi ให้ as a causative compound verb for
making a request + two other words for wanting

> **I** Requesting by wanting – yàak-hâi อยาก ให้
>
> I want you to speak the truth.
>
> ฉัน อยาก ให้ คุณ พูด ความ จริง
> tʃán *yàak-hâi-khun* phûut kwaam-tsing
> I *want-make-you* speak matter-true

- **yàak-hâi** อยาก ให้ *to want, to request*
- **hâi** ให้ is used here together with the verb **yàak** อยาก *to want* in order to request someone do something
- **yàak-hâi** อยาก ให้ expresses a demand or a strong wish. It is commonly used in *casual* speaking
- **yàak-hâi** *to want, to request* is placed before the direct object, here **khun** คุณ *you*
- the action verb, here **phûut** พูด *to speak*, comes after
- the verb **yàak** อยาก must always be followed by the verb, here **hâi** ให้

> **Short form**
>
> อยาก ให้ คุณ พูด ความ จริง
> *yàak-hâi-khun* phûut kwaam-tsing
> *want-make-you* speak matter-true

- the subject, **tʃán** ฉัน *I,* can be dropped when the meaning is understood from the context

Secret 7 – hâi ให้ for *making a request*

2 Formal requesting – tông-gaan-hâi ต้อง การ ให้

I want you to finish it.

ฉัน ต้อง การ ให้ คุณ ทำ ให้ เสร็จ
tʃán *tông-gaan-hâi-khun* tham hâi sèt
I *must-make-you* do make finish

- **tông-gaan hâi** ต้อง การ ให้ *to want, to require, to request*
- **tông-gaan** ต้อง การ *to require* is followed by a verb **hâi** ให้
- **tông-gaan hâi** ต้อง การ ให้ *to request* has the same meaning and is used in the same ways as **yàak-hâi** อยาก ให้ *to request* someone to do something
- however, **tông-gaan hâi** ต้อง การ ให้ is more *formal*, and some books maintain that it is also a more polite way to express needs, demands or requests

Short form

ต้อง การ ให้ ทำ ให้ เสร็จ
tông-gaan-hâi tham hâi sèt
must-task-make do make finish

- the subject, **tʃán** ฉัน *I*, can be dropped when the meaning is understood from the context, also the object can be dropped, here **khun** คุณ you

3 Requesting to get – อยาก ได้

I want to get a pen.

ฉัน อยาก ได้ ปากกา
tʃán *yàak-dâai* pàak-kaa
I *want-get* pen

- **yàak-dâai** อยาก ได้ wanting to get something

- the verb **yàak** อยาก must always be followed by the verb, here **dâai** ได้
- **yàak-dâai** อยาก ได้ is usually followed by a direct object, which is a noun, here **pàak-kaa** ปากกา *a pen*

> **Short form**
>
> อยาก ได้ ปากกา
> *yàak-dâai* pàak-kaa
> *want-get* pen

- the subject, **tʃán** ฉัน *I*, can be dropped when the meaning is understood from the context

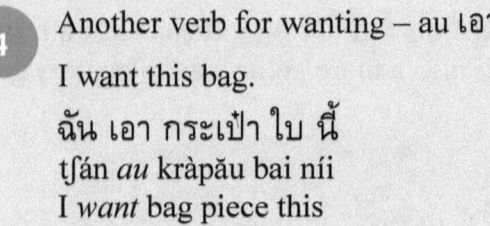

> Another verb for wanting – au เอา
>
> I want this bag.
>
> ฉัน เอา กระเป๋า ใบ นี้
> tʃán *au* kràpǎu bai níi
> I *want* bag piece this

- verb **au** เอา *to want, to take*
- the verb **au** เอา *to want* must always be followed by a noun, here **kràpǎu bai níi** กระเป๋า ใบ นี้ *this bag*, and never by a verb
- **au** เอา *to want* is a more direct way to express to get something compared to **yàak-dâai** อยาก ได้ *to want*
- **au** เอา is directly translated into English as *to take*
- however, **au** เอา in Thai is a more polite way to express wanting than the English verbs *to want* and *to take*. With polite ending particles the above statement could also be translated into English as *I would like to have this bag*

Secret 7 – hâi ให้ for *making a request*

Short form
เอา ใบ นี้
au bai níi

- the subject, **tʃán** ฉัน *I*, can be dropped when the meaning is understood from the context
- also the direct object can be dropped, here **kràpău** กระเป๋า *bag*, when the meaning is understood from the context
- the classifier, **bai** ใบ is enough

B. Understanding hâi ให้ as a causative compound verb for making a request

- **hâi** ให้ as a compound verb for *requesting, wanting, asking*
- **hâi** ให้ as a second element in the compound verb

When we use the term *compound verb in* Thai, we mean that there is a close connection between **hâi** ให้ and the other verb. They are usually not separated.

hâi ให้, together with the other verb in the compound, form one special meaning.

Word order

Put **hâi** ให้ directly after the first verb in the sentence and before the subject to whom the action is directed as follows:

Subject + *yàak-hâi-khun* + verb

I + *want-make-you* + go = I want you to go

a) **hâi** ให้ in the compound when making a request

- **yàak-hâi** อยาก ให้ *to want to* is a simple request

Secret 7 – hâi ให้ for *making a request*

- **yàak-tsà-hâi** อยาก จะ ให้ *would like to* is a more polite way to express a request since it is a bit softer and less direct. It refers to the Future
- **tông-gaan-hâi** ต้อง การ ให้ *to require to* is a formal request and is used in a similar way as **yàak-hâi** อยาก ให้ *to want* but it is a stronger form of expressing wanting
- **khɔ̌ɔ-hâi** ขอ ให้ denotes a polite request from simple *asking* to *wishing, wanting* or *demanding* depending on the situation
- **bɔ̀ɔk-hâi** บอก ให้ *to tell to* is mainly used in connection with the third person

Examples:

1 Simple request

I want you to speak the truth.

ฉัน อยากให้ คุณ พูด ความ จริง
tʃǎn *yàak-hâi-khun* phûut kwaam-tsing
I *want-make-you* speak matter-true

- **yàak-hâi** อยาก ให้ is placed before the direct object, which is here the pronoun **khun** คุณ *you,* who must carry out the action
- the verb **yàak** อยาก *to want* must always be followed by the verb, here **hâi** ให้

2 Polite request

I would like you to speak the truth.

ฉัน อยาก จะ ให้ คุณ พูด ความ จริง นะ คะ
tʃǎn *yàak-tsà-hâi-khun* phûut kwaam-tsing *ná khá*
I *want-will-make-you* speak matter-true *ná khá*

- this is a more polite way to express wanting. In English the translation is *would like to*

Secret 7 – hâi ให้ for *making a request*

- wanting in Thai can be made softer by using the future tense **tsà** จะ *will* and polite ending particles such as **ná khá** นะ คะ
- The future in Thai usually includes plans, intentions and promises. It is not as strong as the English word *will*
- the verb **yàak** อยาก *to want* must always be followed by a verb, here **tsà** จะ

> **3** Formal request
>
> I want you to speak the truth.
>
> ฉัน ต้อง การ ให้ คุณ พูด ความ จริง
> tʃán tôŋ-gaan-hâi-khun phûut kwaam-tsing
> I *must-make-you* speak matter-true

- **tôŋ-gaan hâi** ต้อง การ ให้ is used in formal situations and perhaps also more often in writing
- the verb **tôŋ-gaan** ต้อง การ *to require* can be followed either by a verb or by a noun

b) using **hâi** ให้ alone, without the help of another verb, can be translated into English from *simple wanting to a firm request*. See Secret 4

- when **hâi** ให้ is used alone as a request, it is usually stronger than **yàak-hâi** อยาก ให้
- however, it depends on how the statement is said. Using **hâi** ให้ alone can also mean *to let*
- **hâi** ให้ alone is often used when speaking because it is short and can be understood intuitively
- see more about this in Secret 4

Strictly speaking, verbs like *to ask, to want, to request* are not usually regarded as causative verbs in English. However, in Thai we may count them as causative verbs when used together with **hâi** ให้. For instance, the compound verb construction like **yàak-hâi** อยาก ให้ *to want to* is a way to make someone else do something for you.

We have included in this Secret two other words, which can be translated into English as *to want,* namely **yàak-dâai** อยาก ได้ and **au** เอา. It is important to understand the difference. See language hints later in this Secret.

> **Conclusion**
>
> We may conclude that when **hâi** ให้ is used as a causative compound verb, it is usually placed before a pronoun, someone who needs to carry out the action. As a causative verb **hâi** ให้ points out the person to whom the action is directed.
>
> In this Secret, when **hâi** ให้ is used as a causative compound verb, its semantic boundaries are defined also by the other verb that is used with it.
>
> The other verb together with **hâi** ให้ clarifies the meaning, such as **yàak-hâi** อยาก ให้ *to want to.* The action verb, what type of action is in question, comes after. The word order is Subject + *yàak-hâi-khun* + verb

C. Language hints

We try to explain here subtle differences in Thai, where we in English simply use the verb *to want.*

a) **yàak-hâi** อยาก ให้ *to want*

- **yàak-hâi** อยาก ให้ *to want* expresses an action *away from* the subject or speaker
- someone else must carry out the action
- **yàak-hâi** อยาก ให้ is usually placed before a pronoun followed by the action verb

Secret 7 – hâi ให้ for *making a request*

- **yàak-hâi** อยาก ให้ is a causative compound verb as explained earlier in this section

Examples:

> I want you to speak the truth.
>
> It is not correct to say:
>
> ฉัน / ผม อยาก คุณ พูด ความ จริง
> tʃǎn / phǒm *yàak* khun phûut kwaam-tsing
> I w*ant* you speak matter-true
>
> **Warning**

- using the verb **yàak** อยาก *to want* alone is not possible here
- the verb **yàak** อยาก *to want* must always be followed by another verb
- the verb **yàak** อยาก can't be followed by a direct object
- we need to use here the compound verb **yàak-hâi** อยาก ให้ *to want*
- the correct sentence is tʃǎn / phǒm **yàak-hâi-khun** phûut kwaam-tsing ฉัน / ผม อยาก ให้ คุณ พูด ความ จริง

There are three more words for *wanting* which denote an action *towards* the subject or speaker. Someone is wishing or hoping *to receive* something.

All of these verbs are used differently, and you need to pay close attention in order to choose the right word for the relevant situation.

b) **yàak-dâai** อยาก ได้ *to want to get*

- **yàak-dâai** อยาก ได้ *to want to get* something is usually referring to things
- **yàak-dâai** อยาก ได้ *to want to get* denotes an action *towards* the subject or speaker
- **yàak-dâai** อยาก ได้ *to want* is usually followed by a noun

Examples:

I want to get a car.
ฉัน อยาก ได้ รถ
tʃán *yàak-dâai* rót
I *want-get* car

- **yàak** อยาก *to want* must always be followed by a verb
- here **yàak** อยาก *to want* is followed by the verb **dâai** ได้ *to get*
- **yàak** อยาก *to want* is usually used in the following three ways:
- **yàak-dâai** อยาก ได้ *to want to get* something, usually referring to things and is followed by a direct object (noun)
- **yàak-hâi** อยาก ให้ *to want* or *to request* someone to do something. It is usually followed by a direct object (pronoun)
- **yàak pai** อยาก ไป *to want to go* or **yàak** อยาก + any other action verb

2 I want a car.
It is not correct to say:
ฉัน อยาก รถ
tʃán *yàak* rót
I *want* car

Warning

- **yàak** อยาก *to want* alone reveals hunger
- here the statement would mean that you like cars because they taste good. "I want to eat cars."

Secret 7 – hâi ให้ for *making a request*

> **Correct!**
> I want Japanese food.
> ฉัน อยาก อาหาร ญี่ปุ่น
> tʃán *yàak* aahăan yîipùn
> I *want* food Japan

- here **yàak** อยาก *to want* is followed by a noun
- as usual, there are some exceptions to the rule
- the verb **yàak** อยาก *to want* must always be followed by *another verb* unless it is used in the general sense for something *edible*
- using **yàak** อยาก *to want* this way is not very common even though it is grammatically correct
- it is more common to use the verb **thaan** ทาน *to eat* as follows:

> **Correct!**
> I want to eat Japanese food.
> ฉัน อยาก ทาน อาหาร ญี่ปุ่น
> tʃán *yàak thaan* aahăan yîipùn
> I *want eat* food Japan

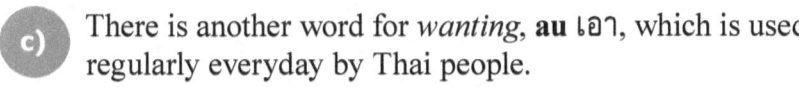

There is another word for *wanting*, **au** เอา, which is used regularly everyday by Thai people.

The difference from **yaak** is that **au** เอา *to want* cannot be followed by a verb, but it must be followed by a noun. So, **au** เอา *to want* can't be followed by the verb **hâi** ให้.

Examples:

1 I want this.
ฉัน เอา อัน นี้
tʃán *au* an-níi
I *want* piece-this

- here **au** เอา *to want* is followed by a pronoun **an-níi** อัน นี้ *this one*. **au** เอา *to want* usually refers to things

2 No, thank you!
ไม่ เอา ค่ะ / ครับ
mâi au khâ / khráp
no want khâ / khráp

- this is a polite way to refuse to buy

d) The fourth word for *wanting* is **tôŋ-gaan** ต้อง การ *to require, to need*. **tôŋ-gaan-hâi** ต้อง การ ให้ is used in the similar way as **yàak-dâai** อยาก ได้

However, **tôŋ-gaan** ต้อง การ can be followed by a *verb* or by a *noun* while **yàak-dâai** อยาก ได้ *to want* and **au** เอา *to want* are followed only by *a noun*.

tôŋ-gaan ต้องการ is more formal than the other two words for wanting. Many Thai learning books point out that **tôŋ-gaan** ต้อง การ *to require, to need* is a more polite way to express wanting.

However, some Thai people feel that it is more demanding and sounds like an order. The **tôŋ** ต้อง means *must*. Perhaps that is one of the reasons it is not used very often by Thais in daily conversation. Thai people like to make a request soft and do not like to give or receive orders.

Secret 7 – hâi ให้ for *making a request*

Examples:

> **1** I want you to speak the truth.
> ฉัน ต้อง การ ให้ คุณ พูด ความ จริง
> tʃǎn *tɔ̂ng-gaan-hâi* khun phûut kwaam-tsing
> I want-make you speak matter-true

- here **tɔ̂ng-gaan** ต้อง การ *to need, to require, to want* is followed by the verb **hâi** ให้

> **2** I want to go.
> ฉัน ต้อง การ ไป
> tʃǎn *tɔ̂ng-gaan* pai
> I want go

- here **tɔ̂ng-gaan** ต้อง การ *to need, to require, to want* is followed by the verb **pai** ไป *to go*

> **3** I want / need money.
> ฉัน ต้อง การ เงิน
> tʃǎn *tɔ̂ng-gaan* ngən
> I *want* money

- here **tɔ̂ng-gaan** ต้อง การ *to need, to require, to want* is followed by a noun **ngən** เงิน *money*

D. Simple advice

The line between general *wanting, would like to* and stating a *request* is often quite small. The request can be made softer by polite particles at the end such as **nɔ̀i** หน่อย *little*, **dûuai** ด้วย *also*, **dâai-mǎi** ได้ไหม *can I*. See more about being polite in Secret 11.

If one wants to make it clear that the statement is a *firm request*, then it can be emphasised with words like **tɔɔn-níi** ตอนนี้ *now* or **than-thii** ทันที *immediately*.

Note also that much depends on the way the statement is said. Exactly the same statement spoken by a *strong western voice* without much feeling may sound like a command, but when spoken with a *soft polite Thai voice,* it would hint of a kind of polite wanting. The same may be true in any language, but it is very much so in Thai. Thai people usually avoid using a strong voice. Therefore, it is always relaxing to sit close to Thai people in the cafeteria.

Secret 8 – hâi ให้ for *firm ordering*

To order!
สั่ง ให้
sàng-hâi

hâi is a very diligent person, who can also give orders – hâi says: "Sometimes we must give orders to get work done."

ให้ เก่ง มาก และ เป็น คน ออกคำสั่ง – ให้ บอก ว่า – บาง ครั้ง เรา ต้อง สั่ง เพื่อ จะ ทำ ให้ งาน เสร็จ

hâi kèng mâak lé pen khon ɔ̀ɔk-kham-sàng – hâi bɔ̀ɔk-wâa – baang-kráng rau tông sàng phûa-tsà tham-hâi ngaan sèt

hâi diligent very and be person issue-word-order – hâi say that – sometime we must order for-will do-make work finish

Secret 8

hâi ให้ as a causative compound verb for *strong, firm ordering*

The word for *ordering* is **sàng** สั่ง *to order something*. Ordering someone to do something is expressed in Thai by the compound verb **sàng-hâi** สั่ง ให้ *to order*.

Other compound verbs like **tông-hâi** ต้อง ให้ *to demand*, **bɔ̀ɔk-hâi** บอก ให้ *to tell*, **rîiak-hâi** เรียก ให้ *to call* may be used depending on the situation.

A. Sentences

hâi ให้ as a causative compound verb for making orders

> **1** Strong, firm ordering – sàng-hâi สั่ง ให้
>
> He ordered me to go to work.
> เขา สั่ง ให้ ฉัน ไป ทำ งาน
> kháu *sàng-hâi tʃán* pai tham-ngaan
> he *order-make I* go do work

- **sàng-hâi** สั่ง ให้ *to order*
- **hâi** ให้ can be used together with the verb **sàng** สั่ง *to order* in order to make the meaning clear
- **sàng-hâi** สั่ง ให้ *to order* is placed before the object, here **tʃán** ฉัน *I*
- what is ordered comes after, here **pai tham-ngaan** ไป ทำ งาน *to go to work*
- **sàng-hâi** สั่ง ให้ *to order* is a strong and formal expression for ordering

> **Short form**
> เขา ให้ ฉัน ไป ทำ งาน
> kháu *hâi-tʃán* pai tham ngaan
> he *make-I* go do work

- the other verb **sàng** สั่ง *to order* can be dropped
- the short form is usually used in spoken Thai
- the short form, where the other verb is omitted, can be considered here a milder request than the complete sentence
- it could also be translated as *to let* or *to request* depending upon how the statement is said

Secret 8 – hâi ให้ for *firm ordering*

2 Ordering by demanding – tông-hâi ต้อง ให้

We demand that everyone respects the law.

เรา ต้อง ให้ ทุก คน เคารพ กฎ หมาย
rau *tông-hâi thúk-khon* khau-róp gòt-măai
we *must-make every-person* regard-respect law-notice

- **tông-hâi** ต้อง ให้ *to demand, to order*
- **tông-hâi** ต้อง ให้ *to demand, to request, to order* expresses the requirement, which must prevail

Short form

เรา ให้ ทุก คน เคารพ กฎ หมาย
rau *hâi thúk-khon* khau-róp gòt-măai
we *make-every-person* regard-respect law-notice

- the verb **tông** ต้อง *must* can be dropped
- the short form, where the other verb is omitted, is a more direct way to express the same
- it can also be translated as *to let* or *to make*. Again much depends on how the statement is said

3 Ordering by telling – bɔ̀ɔk-hâi บอก ให้

Tell him to go and buy some breakfast now.

บอก ให้ เขา ไป ซื้อ อาหาร เช้า ตอน นี้
bɔ̀ɔk-hâi-kháu pai sɯ́ɯ aahăan-tʃáau *tɔɔn-níi*
tell-make-he go buy food-morning *moment-this*

- **bɔ̀ɔk-hâi** บอก ให้ *to tell, to order*
- here **bɔ̀ɔk-hâi** บอก ให้ *to tell, to request, to order* is emphasised by the demanding particle **tɔɔn-níi** ตอน นี้ *now* to make the demand stronger

Short form

ให้ เขา ไป ซื้อ อาหาร เช้า
hâi-kháu pai súu aahăan-tʃáau
make-he go buy food-morning

- the verb **bɔ̀ɔk** บอก *to tell* can be dropped
- the short form, where the other verb is omitted, is a more direct way to express the same idea as in the complete sentence
- this sentence can also be translated into English in several ways depending on the context and how the statement is said such as:
- *let him go and buy some breakfast*
- *request him to go and buy some breakfast*
- *make / have him go and buy some breakfast*

4 Ordering by calling – rîiak-hâi เรียก ให้

Call him and get him to come here immediately.

เรียก ให้ เขา มา นี่ ทัน ที
rîiak-hâi-kháu maa nîi than-thii
call-make-he come here immediately

- **rîiak-hâi** เรียก ให้ *to call, to order*
- here **rîiak-hâi** เรียก ให้ *to call, to order* is used in the similar way as **bɔ̀ɔk-hâi** บอก ให้ *to tell*

Short form

ให้ เขา มา นี่ ทัน ที
hâi-kháu maa nîi than-thii
make-he come here immediately

- the verb **rîiak** เรียก *to call* can be dropped

- note that the shorter form with **hâi** ให้ without **rîiak** เรียก *to call* is similar in meaning to the previous sentence
- here the short form, where the other verb is omitted, can be stronger than the complete sentence because it is a more direct command
- on the other hand, it can also be translated into English as *to let* or *to make him come here*

> **B. Understanding hâi ให้ as a causative compound verb for giving orders**

- **hâi** ให้ as a compound verb for *firm ordering*
- **hâi** ให้ as a second element in the compound verb

When we use the term *compound verb* in Thai, we mean that there is a close connection between **hâi** ให้ and the other verb. They are not usually separated.

hâi ให้ together with the other verb form one clear meaning.

Word order

Put **hâi** ให้ after the other verb in the sentence and before the object to whom the action is directed as follows:

```
Subject + sàng-hâi-tʃán + verb
    he + order-make-I + go = he ordered me to go
```

hâi ให้ together with the verb **sàng** สั่ง *to order* makes the statement strong and clear.

Secret 8 – hâi ให้ for *firm ordering*

Example:

> He ordered me to go to work.
> เขา สั่ง ให้ ฉัน ไป ทำ งาน
> kháu *sàng-hâi-tfǎn* pai tham-ngaan
> he *order-make-I* go do work

- in some cases using **hâi** ให้ *alone* can be translated the same, but it depends upon how the statement is said
- it can also mean *letting* or *requesting*. **hâi** ให้ alone is used mainly in speaking

There are a few other compound verbs for making orders such as:

- **tông-hâi** ต้อง ให้ *to demand*
- **bɔ̀ɔk-hâi** บอก ให้ *to tell*
- **rîiak-hâi** เรียก ให้ *to call*

The above compound verbs are weaker than **sàng-hâi** สั่ง ให้ *to order*. They can also be used for *ordering* depending on the situation. Then the statement is often emphasised by some special words to make it sound more like an order.

Examples:

- **tɔɔn-níi** ตอน นี้ *now*
- **than-thii** ทัน ที *immediately*
- **tsing-tsing** จริงๆ *really*

Strictly speaking verbs like *to demand, to tell, to call* are not usually regarded as causative verbs in English. However, in Thai we may count them as causative verbs when used together with **hâi** ให้. That is a polite way to tell and make someone else to do something.

Conclusion

We may conclude that when **hâi** ให้ is used as a causative compound verb, it is usually placed before a pronoun, someone who needs to carry out the action. As a causative verb **hâi** ให้ points out the person to whom the action is directed.

In this Secret, when **hâi** ให้ is used as a causative compound verb, its semantic boundaries are defined also by the other verb that is used together with it.

For Thai people **hâi** ให้ is one word, and the meaning is *to give*. However, its semantic boundary is much wider than the usage of the English word *to give*. Therefore, we need to use several different English words to grasp the correct meaning of **hâi** ให้. See more about the term "semantic boundary" and other grammar terms at the end of this book.

The other verb together with **hâi** ให้ clarifies the meaning, such as **sàng-hâi** สั่ง ให้ *to order*. The action verb, what type of action is in question, comes after. The word order is Subject + *sàng-hâi-tɕán* + verb.

C. Language hints

These four words, **sàng** สั่ง *to order*, **tɔ̂ng** ต้อง *must*, **bɔ̀ɔk** บอก *to tell* and **rîiak** เรียก *to call* behave somewhat differently grammatically when used alone without the verb **hâi** ให้.

sàng สั่ง *to order* can be used alone, but the meaning is different.

The verb **sàng** สั่ง *to order* can be used alone for ordering something, it is often used for food or drinks in the restaurant.

The waiter may ask you:

Secret 8 – hâi ให้ for *firm ordering*

1 Have you ordered?
สั่ง หรือ ยัง
sàng rǔɯ-yang
order or-yet

You can reply:

1.1 Not yet!
ยัง ค่ะ / ครับ
yang khâ / khráp
yet, khâ / khráp

or

1.2 I have already ordered, thank you!
สั่ง แล้ว ค่ะ / ครับ
sàng lɛ́ɛu khâ / khráp
order already khâ / khráp

1.3 He ordered me to go to work.   **Warning**
It is not correct to say:
เขา สั่ง ฉัน ไป ทำ งาน
kháu *sàng* tʃán pai tham ngaan
he *order* I go do work

- in spoken Thai, however, you may sometimes hear people use this style of language

- the correct sentence is: kháu **sàng-hâi** tʃán pai tham ngaan เขา สั่ง ให้ ฉัน ไป ทำงาน

The following verbs are not usually used alone

Secret 8 – hâi ให้ for *firm ordering*

2 We demand that everyone respects the law.   **Warning**

It is not correct to say:

เรา ต้อง ทุก คน เคารพ กฎ หมาย
rau *tông* thúk-kon khau-róp gòt-măai
we *must* every person regard-respect law-notice

- **tông** ต้อง *must* needs to be followed by a verb **hâi** ให้
- therefore it would be totally wrong to leave **hâi** ให้ out in the above sentence
- the correct sentence is: rau **tông-hâi** thúk-kon khau-róp gòt-măai
  เรา ต้อง ให้ ทุก คน เคารพ กฎ หมาย

3 Tell him to go buy some food now.   **Warning**

It is not correct to say:

บอก เขา ไป ซื้อ อาหาร ตอน นี้
bɔ̀ɔk kháu pai sɯ́ɯ aahăan tɔɔn-níi
tell he go buy food moment-this

- in spoken Thai, however, you may hear people use this style of language
- using the verb **bɔ̀ɔk** บอก *to tell* alone is OK, but this means that the speaker is not worried about being 100% correct
- the correct sentence is: **bɔ̀ɔk-hâi** kháu pai sɯ́ɯ aa-hăan tʃáau tɔɔn-níi บอก เขา ให้ ไป ซื้อ อาหาร เช้า ตอน นี้

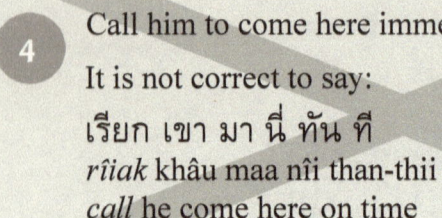

4 Call him to come here immediately.
It is not correct to say:
เรียก เขา มา นี่ ทัน ที
rîiak khâu maa nîi than-thii
call he come here on time

- **rîiak** เรียก *to call* is not usually used alone
- in spoken Thai, however, you may hear people use this type of expressio0n
- using the verb **rîiak** เรียก *to call* alone is OK, but this means that the speaker is not worried about being 100% correct
- the correct sentence is: **rîiak-hâi** khâu maa nîi than-thii เรียก ให้ เขา มา นี่ ทัน ที

Ending particles can change the meaning:

- **sàng-hâi** สั่ง ให้ *to order* is the strongest compound verb for *giving orders*
- **bɔ̀ɔk-hâi** บอก ให้ *to tell* with words such as **tɔɔn-níi** ตอนนี้ *now* or **than-thii** ทันที *immediately* is used to express a *strong request* or *milder order*
- **bɔ̀ɔk-hâi** บอก ให้ *to tell* with polite request particles such as **nɔ̀i** หน่อย *little* or **dâai-măi** ได้ ไหม *can-you* express a *polite* request since the statement gives the other more choice

D. Simple advice

The Thai language needs to be learned from phrases and sentences rather than single words, since the same words are used in different ways in different sentences. Often there is no available grammatical explanation as to why. **hâi** ให้ is a very good example of this type of word.

In addition, there are many words, which are not used at all in daily speech, but they are in the dictionary. Some words are never used alone but only in combination with other words. This you need to learn in practice.

Thais often have difficulty understanding the meaning of one word without a context, however when the word is used in a sentence in the correct way, the meaning is clear.

To lend
ให้ ยืม
hâi-yuum

hâi meets verbs *to borrow, to know* and *to see*. hâi says: "I enjoy being a friend with this group of verbs. We often play together. I would like you to come and play with us."

ให้ เจอ คำ กริยา "ให้ ยืม" "ให้ รู้" และ "ให้ ดู" – ให้ บอก ว่า – ฉัน ชอบ เป็น เพื่อน กับ คำ กริยา เหล่า นี้ – เรา เล่น ด้วย กัน บ่อยๆ – ฉัน อยาก ให้ คุณ มา เล่น ด้วย กัน

hâi tsəə kham griyaa *hâi-yuum hâi-rúu* lé *hâi-duu* – hâi bɔ̀ɔk-wâa – tʃǎn tʃɔ̂ɔp pen phûuan kàp kham-griyaa làu níi – rau lên dûuai kan bɔ̀i-bɔ̀i – tʃǎn yàak-hâi khun maa lên dûuai kan

hâi meet word verb let-borrow let-know and let-see – hâi tell that – I like be friend with word verb group this – we play together often-often – I want-make you come play together with

Secret 9

hâi ให้ and some *special verbs*

With some common verbs **hâi** ให้ can be placed as a first element in the compound verb.

There are a few special verbs, which are used in this way with **hâi** ให้. Good examples are:

hâi-rúu	ให้ รู้	to let know
hâi-duu	ให้ ดู	to let look
hâi-yʉʉm	ให้ ยืม	to lend, to let borrow

A. Sentences

hâi ให้ placed before some special verbs

> **I** Lending, borrowing – hâi-yuum ให้ ยืม
>
> He let me borrow his umbrella.
>
> เขา ให้ ฉัน ยืม ร่ม ของ เขา
> kháu *hâi-tʃán-yuum* rôm khɔ̌ɔng kháu
> he *let-I-borrow* umbrella of he

- **hâi-yuum** ให้ ยืม *to lend, to let borrow*

- the object **tʃán** ฉัน *I* is placed between the verb **hâi** ให้ *to let* and **yuum** ยืม *to borrow*

- note that in Thai there is not actually the word *to lend*. It is expressed by the verb compound **hâi-yuum** ให้ ยืม *to let borrow, to lend*

- the above sentence could also be translated as *he lent me his umbrella*

> **Short form**
>
> เขา ให้ ยืม ร่ม เขา
> kháu *hâi-yuum* rôm kháu
> he *let-borrow* umbrella he

- the object **tʃán** ฉัน *I* can be left out when understood from the context

- also the possessive form **khɔ̌ɔng** ของ *of* can be left out, and the meaning doesn't change

> **2** Letting know – hâi-rúu ให้ รู้
>
> I'll let you know.
>
> ฉัน จะ ให้ คุณ รู้
> tʃán tsà hâi-khun-rúu
> I will *let-you-know*

- **hâi-rúu** ให้รู้ *to let know*
- the object **khun** คุณ *you* is placed between the verbs **hâi** ให้ *to let* and **rúu** รู้ *to know*

> **Short form**
>
> จะ ให้ คุณ รู้
> tsà hâi-khun-rúu
> will *let-you-know*

- the subject **tʃán** ฉัน *I* can be left out

> **3** Letting look – hâi-duu ให้ ดู
>
> Let me have a look!
>
> ขอ ให้ ฉัน ดู หน่อย
> khɔ̌ɔ hâi-tʃán-duu nɔ̀i
> ask *let-I-see* little

- **hâi-duu** ให้ ดู *to look*
- the object **tʃán** ฉัน *I* is placed between the verb **hâi** ให้ *to let* and **duu** ดู *to look*

Short form

ขอ ดู หน่อย
khɔ̌ɔ *duu* nɔ̀i
ask *see* little

- the object **tʃán** ฉัน *I* and the word **hâi** ให้ can be left out, and the meaning is the same or similar. However, the expression is shorter and more direct

B. Understanding hâi ให้ and some special verbs

- **hâi** ให้ can be placed before *some special common verbs*
- **hâi** ให้ as the first element in the compound verb

Word order
Put **hâi** ให้ before the object to whom the action is directed followed by the verb as below.

Subject + *hâi-khun-yɯɯm* + object

I + *let-you-borrow* + umbrella = I let you borrow an umbrella.

Previously, we saw how **hâi** ให้ was used *as a second element* in a compound structure and was placed after the other verb such as in **yɔɔm-hâi** ยอม ให้ *to let, to allow, to give up*.

With some common verbs **hâi** ให้ is placed as a first element in the compound structure.

The most common verbs are:

hâi-yɯɯm	ให้ ยืม	*to lend, to let borrow*
hâi-duu	ให้ ดู	*to show, to let look*
hâi-hěn	ให้ เห็น	*to see, to let see*
hâi-fang	ให้ ฟัง	*to listen, to let hear*
hâi-tʃâu	ให้ เช่า	*to let, to let rent*

Secret 9 – hâi ให้ and some special verbs

Conclusion

We may conclude that with some verbs **hâi** ให้ can be placed as a first element in the compound structure.

Compare this Secret with the Secret 4 *to allow, to request, to make*. The structure is the same. However, the words used are different, and consequently the meaning and the tone of the language are different. Here there is a closer connection between **hâi** ให้ and the other verb. Therefore we regard it as a compound structure.

These types of verbs together with **hâi** ให้ usually convey permissive meanings such as *to let, to permit* or *to allow*.

C. Language hints

hâi ให้ can be placed either as a first element or as a second element in a compound structure

a) With some verbs **hâi** ให้ is placed as a *first element* in the compound

Examples:

1 He has a story to tell.
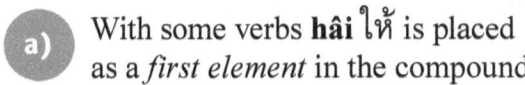
kháu mii rûang tsà lâu *hâi-fang*
he have story will tell *let-hear*

- here **hâi** ให้ is placed as a *first element* in the compound before the verb **fang** ฟัง *to listen, to hear*

> **1.1** He has a story to tell.
> It is not correct to say:
> เขา มี เรื่อง จะ เล่า ฟัง ให้
> kháu mii rûuang tsà lâu *fang-hâi*
> he have story will tell *hear-let*
>
> **Warning**

- here it is not correct to place **hâi** ให้ as a second element in the compound verb
- with **fang** ฟัง **hâi** ให้ must be placed as a first element in the compound

b) **hâi** ให้ is often placed as a *second element* in the compound verb

Examples:

> **1** He allowed me to go on the trip.
> เขา ยอม ให้ ฉัน ไป เที่ยว
> kháu *yɔɔm-hâi* tʃán pai thîiau
> he *allow-let* I go trip

- **yɔɔm-hâi** ยอม ให้ *to permit / to allow*

> **1.1** He allowed me to go on the trip.
> It is not correct to say:
> เขา ให้ ยอม ฉัน ไป เที่ยว
> kháu *hâi-yɔɔm* tʃán pai thîiau
> he *let-allow* I go trip
>
> **Warning**

- with **yɔɔm** ยอม **hâi** ให้ must be placed as a second element in the compound

c) Learn to separate **hâi** ให้ as *to let* and *to give* in English.

Secret 9 – hâi ให้ and some special verbs

Examples:

> **1**
> I will let you rent my car.
> ผม จะ ให้ คุณ เช่า รถ ผม
> phŏm tsà *hâi-khun-tʃâu* rót phŏm
> I will *let-you-rent* car I

- when the pronoun, here **khun** คุณ *you*, follows the verb **hâi** ให้ the meaning is *to let*

> **1.1**
> He has a house for rent.
> เขา มี บ้าน ให้ เช่า
> kháu mii bâan *hâi-tʃâu*
> he have house *let-rent*

- in this context **hâi-tʃâu** ให้ เช่า is better translated into English as *for rent*

> **2**
> I will give you my car.
> ผม จะ ให้ รถ ผม กับ คุณ
> phŏm tsà *hâi-rót* phŏm kàp khun
> I will *give-car* I with you

- when the noun, here **rót** รถ *car*, follows **hâi** ให้ then the meaning is *to give*
- this sentence can also be translated into English as *I'll give my car to you*
- see more about this structure in Secrets 1 and 2

d) Note also that there are two ways to form a genitive, possessive form in Thai

- the possessive form is expressed by the preposition **khɔ̌ɔng** ของ *of*

The structure is as follows:

> car + khɔ̌ɔng ของ + you
>
>> Your car.
>>
>> รถ ของ คุณ
>> rót *khɔ̌ɔng* khun
>> car *of* you

Short form

> car + you
>
>> Your car.
>>
>> รถ คุณ
>> rót khun
>> car you

- the word **khɔ̌ɔng** ของ can be omitted. The short form is often preferred in speaking
- note also that the word **khɔ̌ɔng** ของ has another meanings as well. It is used for *things, stuff, possessions*

Example:

>> My stuff.
>>
>> ของ ของ ผม
>> khɔ̌ɔng *khɔ̌ɔng* phǒm
>> stuff *of* I

D. Simple advice

Thai people understand the verb **hâi** ให้ from the context and use it very intuitively. It can be translated into English in several different ways. However, if you ask Thai people about the meaning of **hâi** ให้, they will most likely tell you that it means *to give*.

In addition, **hâi** ให้ can often be translated into English as *to let* or *to make*. The word **hâi** ให้ is a verb but the translation into English can also include words like *for, to* or *until*.

We have already demonstrated that, apart from using **hâi** ให้ as a main verb in the sentence meaning *to give, to let* or *to make*, it can also be used together with several other verbs as a *compound verb*. The meaning is also then coloured by the other verb. Hence, the meaning has greater clarity than when using **hâi** ให้ alone.

Generally, we may conclude that the meaning of **hâi** ให้, whatever the translation into English is, can usually be understood as *to give* or as a request or command towards *someone else, having* or *making someone to do something.*

PART III

hâi ให้ and offering help and being polite

Secret 10 – hâi ให้ and offering help and being polite

Let me
ให้ ฉัน
hâi tʃán

hâi is a very polite person. hâi says: "If you have any problems, let me help you. I can do it for you."

ให้ เป็น คน ที่ สุภาพ มาก – ให้ บอก ว่า – ถ้า คุณ มี ปัญหา อะไร ให้ ฉัน ช่วย นะ – ฉัน ทำ ให้ ได้

hâi pen khon thîi sùphâap mâak – hâi bɔ̀ɔk-wâa – thâa khun mii panhăa arai – hâi tʃán tʃûuai ná – tʃán tham-hâi dâai

hâi be person that polite very – hâi tell that – if you have problem what – let I help ná – I do-make can

Secret 10

hâi ให้ and *offering help*

Offering help is usually expressed with **hâi** ให้ *let me, allow me*. Thai people are generally very polite and ready to offer help. Learning the proper way to express yourself is important in ensuring you do not sound harsh or intrusive.

A. Sentences

Offering help

> **1** Could I help you – hâi tʃán tʃûuai ให้ ฉัน ช่วย
>
> Could I help you or not?
>
> ให้ ฉัน ช่วย รึ เปล่า
> *hâi-tʃán-tʃûuai rʉ́-plàau*
> let-I-help or-not

- **hâi tʃán** ให้ ฉัน *let me...*
- **hâi** ให้ is placed before the pronoun, here **tʃán** ฉัน *I*, followed by the action verb, here **tʃûuai** ช่วย *to help*
- the question particle **rʉ́-plàau** รึ เปล่า is usually placed at the end of the sentence

> **Short form**
>
> ให้ ช่วย รึ เปล่า
> *hâi-tʃûuai rʉ́-plàau*
> let-help or-not

- in spoken Thai the pronoun, **tʃán** ฉัน *I*, can be dropped

> **2** Let me do it – hâi tʃán tham-hâi ให้ ฉัน ทำ ให้
>
> Let me do it for you, okay?
>
> ให้ ฉัน ทำ ให้ เอา ไหม
> *hâi-tʃán-tham-hâi au mái*
> let-I-do-make want question

- **hâi tʃán** ให้ ฉัน *let me...*
- **hâi** ให้ is placed before the pronoun, here **tʃán** ฉัน *I*, followed by the action verb, here **tham** ทำ *to do*

Secret 10 – hâi ให้ and *offering help*

- the question particle **au mái** เอา ไหม is usually placed at the end of the sentence

> **Short form**
>
> ทำ ให้ เอา ไหม
> *tham-hâi* au-mái
> *do-make* want-question

- in speaking, the first part of the sentence **hâi tʃán** ให้ ฉัน *let me,* can be dropped

> **3** Let him help – hâi kháu tʃûuai ให้ เขา ช่วย
>
> Would you like him to help you?
>
> ให้ เขา ช่วย ได้ ไหม
> *hâi-kháu-tʃûuai* dâai-mái
> *let-he-help* can-question

- **hâi kháu** ให้ เขา *let him...*
- **hâi** ให้ is placed before the pronoun, here **kháu** เขา *he,* followed by the action verb, here **tʃûuai** ช่วย *to help*
- the question particle **dâai-mái** ได้ ไหม is placed at the end of the sentence

> **Short form**
>
> ให้ เขา ช่วย ไหม
> *hâi-kháu-tʃûuai* mái
> *let-he-help* question

- when we use a **mái** ไหม question instead of a **dâai-mái** ได้ ไหม question at the end of the sentence, the statement turns into a direct question: *Will you let him help you?*

B. Understanding hâi ให้ and offering help

- **hâi** ให้ and offering help *let me, let him...*
- **hâi** ให้ is placed before the pronoun, who is offering help

Word order

Put **hâi** ให้ *to let* before the subject who is offering help followed by the helping word.

> *hâi-tʃán-verb* + pronoun + question word
>
> *let-I-help* + you + OK? = let me help you, OK?

The statement is usually finished with a question word like:

rú-plàau	รึเปล่า	or not?
au-mái	เอาไหม	do you want?
dâai-mái	ได้ไหม	can I?
mái	ไหม	question word

Conclusion

Offering help is commonly expressed by placing the verb **hâi** ให้ *to let* before the pronoun, who is offering help, followed by the action verb.

The structure is seemingly similar in English, **hâi tʃán** ให้ฉัน *let me, allow me...*

C. Language hints

Offering help and replying

a) Offering help can also be turned into a direct suggestion without a question word as follows:

Secret 10 – hâi ให้ and *offering help*

Let me help you!
ให้ ฉัน ช่วย
hâi-tʃǎn-tʃûuai
let-I-help

b) There are several different ways to respond when you have been offered help.

Here we have a few most common responses.

1 That would be nice. Thank you!
ก็ ดี นะ ขอบ คุณ ค่ะ / ครับ
gɔ̂ɔ-dii-ná – khɔ̀ɔp-khun khâ / khráp
well-good-ná – thank you khâ / khráp!

- this is polite and can be used in many situations

2 Never mind!
ไม่ เป็น ไร ค่ะ / ครับ
mâi-pen-rai khâ / khráp!
no-be-what khâ / khráp!

- this is polite and can be used in many situations

3 That would be OK.
ช่วย ก็ ดี
tʃûuai-gɔ̂ɔ-dii
help-well-good

- this kind of expression is often used with friends!

4 Yes, please!
ค่ะ / ครับ
khâ / khráp!

- often polite ending particles **khâ** ค่ะ or **khráp** ครับ can be used as a positive reply, and nothing else is needed

D. Simple advice

If you have difficulties being understood by Thais, see if you can improve your language skills, and identify your weak points.

1. Learn to pronounce short vowels short and long vowels long. In English it does not matter that much but in Thai it is very important.

2. Learn to pronounce *unaspirated* consonant sounds at the beginning of a word correctly. In English similar sounds, as P in the word Peter, are always pronounced *aspirated* in the beginning of the word. It is essential to make a distinction. See more about this and end sounds at the end of this book.

3. Learn to use tones correctly. In other words learn to sing in Thai.

4. Learn to use the right word in the right situation. Start using most common words with confidence and be sensitive to the Thai culture. You will get it!

If you are not sure about Thai sounds, you may benefit from reading the book *22 Secrets of Learning Thai – Complete Guide to Sounds, Tones and Thai Writing System*.

I would like you to...
อยาก ให้... หน่อย ได้ ไหม
yàak-hâi... nɔ̀i dâai-mǎi

hâi is a person, who would like to feel good and have fun with everyone. hâi says: "When you want something, do not forget to use polite language like this. 'Could I have some water, please?'"

ให้ เป็น คน ที่ อยาก จะ ให้ ความ รู้ สึก ดีๆ และ ความ สนุก สนาน กับ ทุกคน – ให้ บอก ว่า – ถ้า คุณ อยาก ได้ อะไร อย่า ลืม ใช้ คำ สุภาพ แบบ นี้ – ขอ น้ำ ให้ หน่อย นะ คะ

hâi pen khon thîi yàak-tsà hâi khwaam-rúu-sùk dii-dii lɛ́ khwaam-sànùk-sànǎan kàp thúk-khon – hâi bɔ̀ɔk-wâa – thâa khun yàak-dâai arai yàa lɯɯm tʃái kham sùphâap bɛ̀ɛp níi – "khɔ̌ɔ náam hâi nɔ̀i ná khá"

hâi is person that want-will give matter-know-happy good-good and matter-happy-fun with every person – hâi tell that – if you want-get what no forget use word polite like this – ask water for little ná khá

SECRET 11

hâi ให้ and *polite asking*

Polite asking is usually expressed with the patterns **khɔ̌ɔ-hâi** ขอ ให้ *to ask* with a polite end particle at the end of the statement.

Other compound verbs, like **yàak-hâi** อยาก ให้ *to want* and **bɔ̀ɔk-hâi** บอก ให้ *to tell* may be used depending on the situation.

A. Sentences

Being polite

1 Polite asking – khɔ̌ɔ-hâi... ná khá ขอ ให้... นะ คะ

I would like you to wash your hands first.

ฉัน ขอ ให้ คุณ ล้าง มือ ก่อน นะ คะ
tʃán *khɔ̌ɔ-hâi-khun* láang mɯɯ kɔ̀ɔn *ná khá*
I *ask-make-you* wash hand first *ná khá!*

- **khɔ̌ɔ-hâi... ná khá** ขอ ให้... นะ คะ *polite asking*
- the phrase **tʃán khɔ̌ɔ-hâi khun** ฉัน ขอ ให้ คุณ *I ask you to...* is better translated here into English as *I would like you to...*

Short form

ล้าง มือ ก่อน นะ คะ
láang mɯɯ kɔ̀ɔn *ná khá*
wash hand first *ná khá!*

- when the meaning is understood from the context, the first part of the sentence can be dropped, which is common when speaking
- here the meaning changes a little to become more direct and sounds more like a soft command, *please wash your hands first*

2 Polite asking by wanting – yàak-hâi... nɔ̀i dâai-mǎi
อยาก ให้... หน่อย ได้ ไหม

Would you move a little!

ฉัน อยาก ให้ คุณ ขยับ หน่อย ได้ ไหม
tʃán *yàak-hâi-khun* khàyàp *nɔ̀i dâai-mǎi*
I *want-make-you* move *little can-question*

Secret 11 – hâi ให้ and *being polite*

- **yàak-hâi... nɔ̀i dâai-mǎi** อยาก ให้... หน่อย ได้ ไหม *polite wanting*

- the phrase **tɟán yàak-hâi khun** ฉัน อยาก ให้ คุณ *I want you to...* is better translated here into English as *Would you...*

- we have here two polite ending particles, which make the statement softer, namely **nɔ̀i** หน่อย *little* and **dâai-mǎi** ได้ ไหม *could you*

> **Short form**
>
> ขยับ หน่อย ค่ะ
> khàyàp *nɔ̀i khâ*
> move *little khá*

- when the meaning is understood from the context, the first part of the sentence can be dropped, which is common when speaking

- without **yàak-hâi** อยาก ให้ the meaning changes to become more direct and sounds a bit like an order, *please move a little!*

3 Polite asking by telling – **bɔ̀ɔk-hâi... dûuai**
บอก ให้... ด้วย

Please tell him to finish it.

บอก ให้ เขา ทำ ให้ เสร็จ ด้วย นะ คะ
bɔ̀ɔk-hâi-kháu tham hâi sèt *dûuai ná khá*
tell-make-he do make finish *also ná khá*

- **bɔ̀ɔk-hâi...dûuai ná khá** บอก ให้... ด้วย นะ คะ *polite telling*

- here the third party request is made more soft and polite by the polite ending particle **ná khá** นะ คะ at the end of the statement

- note that **dûuai** ด้วย *also* here is a polite ending particle. It is commonly used in many situations to soften the request

> **Short form**
> ให้ เขา ทำ ให้ เสร็จ ด้วย
> *hâi-kháu* tham hâi sèt *dûuai*
> *make-he* do make finish *also*

- when the meaning is understood from the context, the first part of the sentence can be dropped, which is common when speaking
- the meaning changes a little to become more direct and sounds more like a soft command
- by using **hâi** ให้ alone the meaning changes to *have him do...* or *make him do...*
- note that this statement could also mean *let him...* or *request him...* depending on the context, and how the statement is said

B. Understanding hâi ให้ and being polite

- **hâi** ให้ and being polite, *may I, can I, please*
- **hâi** ให้ as a second element in the compound verb

Word order
Put **hâi** ให้ after the other verb in the compound and before the object to whom action is directed as follows:

> Subject + *khɔ̌ɔ-hâi-khun* + verb + polite particle
>
> I + *ask-make-you* + move + ná khá / khráp =
> I would like you to move a little

Common verbs used with **hâi** ให้ for polite asking:

- **khɔ̌ɔ-hâi** ขอ ให้ *to ask*
- **yàak-hâi** อยาก ให้ *to want*
- **bɔ̀ɔk-hâi** บอก ให้ *to tell*

Secret 11 – hâi ให้ and *being polite*

hâi ให้ is often used in connection with some sort of request or demand. Therefore, it is important to use polite particles in order to not sound too harsh. The request can be softened by the polite request particles such as:

nɔ̀i	หน่อย	*little*
dûuai	ด้วย	*also*
dâai-măi	ได้ไหม	*can you?*
khâ	ค่ะ	*polite particle for women*
khráp	ครับ	*polite particle for men*
ná	นะ	*ok?*

Example:

> I would like you to speak the truth.
>
> ผม ขอ ให้ คุณ พูด ความ จริง นะ ครับ
> phŏm *khɔ̌ɔ-hâi-khun* phûut kwaam-tsing *ná khráp*
> I *ask-make-you* speak matter-true *ná khráp*

- this is a polite way to express wanting, but the feeling is more like *asking* in Thai, while the translation into English would be *I would like you to...*

Strictly speaking, verbs like *to ask, to want, to tell* are not usually regarded as causative verbs in English. However, in Thai we may count them as causative verbs when used together with **hâi** ให้. This is a polite way *to make* or *have* someone else do something.

Often Thais prefer to give "indirect orders". That is to say if you can make your order sound like an invitation, then perhaps it will be accepted more easily.

Conclusion

We may conclude that **hâi** ให้ is often used as a causative compound verb. It is usually placed before a pronoun, someone who needs to carry out the action. As a causative compound verb **hâi** ให้ points out the person to whom the action is directed.

In this Secret, when **hâi** ให้ is used as a causative compound verb, its semantic boundaries are defined also by the other verb it is used together with.

For Thai people **hâi** ให้ is one word, and the meaning is to *give*. However, its semantic boundary is much wider than the usage of the English word *to give*. Therefore, we need to use several different English words to grasp the correct meaning of **hâi** ให้. See more about the term "semantic boundary" and other grammar terms at the end of this book.

The other verb together with **hâi** ให้ clarifies the meaning, such as **khɔ̌ɔ-hâi** ขอให้ *to ask, to want*. The action verb, what type of action is in question, comes later in the sentence. The word order is Subject + *khɔ̌ɔ-hâi-khun* + verb + polite particle

The causative meaning of **hâi** ให้ is also changed and softened here by the polite ending particles.

Without *polite particles* the request would sound too harsh. Compare this Secret with Secret 6 *to request*. The only difference is that here we use polite ending particles. Also when speaking, the tone of the voice is softer and more polite.

C. Language hints

Polite particles in Thai are usually placed at the end of the sentence. However, we have three more words to express politeness. They are usually placed at the beginning of the sentence.

Two of these words are somewhat more formal and are often used in writing and formal situations such as government offices and business relations. They are **kàrúnaa** กรุณา *please, kindly* and **dâai-pròot** ได้โปรด *please*. **tʃûuai** ช่วย *please*, is also used in speaking and informal situations.

Consider the following statements:

> **1** Please move a little, will you?
> ช่วย ขยับ หน่อย ได้ไหม
> *tʃûuai khàyàp nɔ̀i dâai-mǎi*
> *please move little can-question*

- **tʃûuai** ช่วย *please*
- **tʃûuai** ช่วย *please* is a very polite way to express a request. It is placed at the beginning of the statement
- being polite may be strengthened also by the polite particles
- **tʃûuai** ช่วย *please* can be used in ordinary daily conversation as well as in more formal situations

> **2** Please wash your hands first.
> กรุณา ล้าง มือ ก่อน นะ คะ / ครับ
> *kàrúnaa láang mɯɯ kɔ̀ɔn ná khá / khráp!*
> *please wash hand first ná khá / khráp!*

- **kàrúnaa** กรุณา *please, kindly*
- **kàrúnaa** กรุณา *please* is often used in formal situations. It is placed at the beginning of the statement

- being polite may be also strengthened by the polite ending particles
- The above expression could very well be used in government offices and formal situations.

> **3** Please make him finish it.
> ได้ โปรด ให้ เขา ทำ ให้ เสร็จ นะ คะ / ครับ
> *dâai-pròot hâi* kháu tham *hâi* sèt ná *khá / khráp*
> get-please let he do let finish khá / khráp

- **dâai-pròot** ได้ โปรด *please*
- **dâai-pròot** ได้ โปรด *please* is a very formal and not common way to express politeness in speaking
- **pròot** โปรด *please* is often used, however, when making announcements for example at the airports, **pròot sâap** โปรด ทราบ *Please note that... Please be informed that...*

D. Simple advice

In Thai, the polite particles are very important. The above polite request particles make a statement or request more polite and less demanding. If these polite words and polite ending particles are ignored, the above sentences would sound harsh and more like an order.

> Please learn to use these polite words and polite ending particles well in your daily conversation with Thai people. If you do, you will be more easily accepted and welcomed into the Thai society.

Other particles such as **tɔɔn-níi** ตอนนี้ *now* **than-thii** ทันที *immediately* make a statement sound more demanding.

Thai people are hard working people, who also want to have fun while working. They do not like to receive direct orders or to be pushed or forced to do something. See if you can make your request sound like a "polite asking". If you can, then you have understood the Thai way. This is an important point to understand if you have a superior position in the work place with Thais.

Secret 12 – hâi ให้ with *persuasion* and *invitation*

To persuade
ชวน ให้
tʃuuan-hâi

hâi likes to make friends with everyone. Sometimes she likes to persuade friends to go out with her. hâi says: "I want you to go out with me. Where would you like to go? Would it be nice to go to the beach?"

ให้ ชอบ เป็น เพื่อน กับ ทุก คน – บาง ครั้ง ชอบ ชวน ให้ เพื่อน ไป ด้วย – ให้ บอก ว่า – ฉัน อยาก ชวน ให้ คุณ ไป เที่ยว กับ ฉัน – คุณ ชอบ ไป ที่ ไหน – ไป ที่ ชายหาด ดี ไหม

hâi tʃɔ̂ɔp pen phɯ̂ɯan kàp thúk khon – baang khráng tʃɔ̂ɔp tʃuuan-hâi phɯ̂ɯan pai dûuai – hâi bɔ̀ɔk-wâa – tʃán yàak tʃuuan-hâi khun pai thîiau kàp tʃán – khun tʃɔ̂ɔp pai thîi nǎi? pai thîi tʃaai-hàat dii mǎi

hâi like be friend with every person – some time like persuade-let friend go with – hâi tell that – I want persuade-let you go tour with I – you like go place where – go place-beach good is it

SECRET 12

hâi ให้ and *persuading, asking, inviting*

When urging someone to do something, the verb construction, **tʃuuan-hâi** ชวน ให้ *to persuade* is used in Thai.

Other compound verbs like **khɔ̌ɔ-hâi** khɔ̌ɔ-hâi ขอ ให้ *to ask* and **tʃəən-hâi** เชิญ ให้ *to invite* may also be used depending on the situation.

Secret 12 – hâi ให้ with *persuasion* and *invitation*

A. Sentences

Persuading, asking, inviting

> **1**
>
> Persuading – tʃuuan-hâi ชวน ให้
>
> I want to persuade you to stay with me next week.
>
> ฉัน อยาก ชวน ให้ คุณ อยู่ กับ ฉัน อาทิตย์ หน้า นะ คะ
> tʃán yàak *tʃuuan-hâi-khun* yùu kàp tʃán aathít-nâa
> *ná khá*
> I want *persuade-make-you* stay with I week next
> *ná khá*

- **tʃuuan-hâi** ชวน ให้ *to persuade*
- **hâi** ให้ can be used together with the verb **tʃuuan** ชวน *to persuade*
- the polite particle **khâ** ค่ะ is used at the end to make the statement softer

> **Short form**
>
> อยู่ กับ ฉัน อาทิตย์ หน้า นะ คะ
> *yùu* kàp tʃán aathít-nâa *ná khá*
> **stay** with I week next *ná khá*

- the action verb **yùu** อยู่ *to stay* can be used alone without **tʃuuan-hâi** ชวน ให้ *to persuade*
- when the meaning is understood from the context, the object, here **tʃán** ฉัน *I*, can also be dropped
- the meaning changes here to become more direct and sounds more like a suggestion, *Stay with me week next*

Secret 12 – hâi ให้ with *persuasion* and *invitation*

2 Persuading by asking – khɔ̌ɔ-hâi... ná khá
ขอ ให้... นะ คะ

Would you finish it first?
ฉัน ขอ ให้ คุณ ทำ ให้ เสร็จ ก่อน นะ คะ
tʃán *khɔ̌ɔ-hâi-khun* tam hâi-sèt kɔ̀ɔn *ná khá*
I *ask-make-you* do make-finish first *ná khá*

- **khɔ̌ɔ-hâi... ná khá** ขอ ให้... นะ คะ *to ask / to persuade*
- **hâi** ให้ can be used together with the verb **khɔ̌ɔ-hâi** ขอ ให้ *to ask*
- the polite ending particle **ná khá** นะ คะ is used at the end to make the statement a bit softer
- **khɔ̌ɔ-hâi... ná khá** ขอ ให้... นะ คะ could be translated into English as *polite asking* or *polite persuading* depending on the situation. See also Secret 11

Short form

ทำ ให้ เสร็จ ก่อน นะ คะ
tham hâi-sèt kɔ̀ɔn *ná khá*
do make-finish first *ná khá*

- the action verb **tham** ทำ *to do* can be used alone without **khɔ̌ɔ-hâi** ขอ ให้ *to ask*
- when the meaning is understood from the context, the object, here **tʃán** ฉัน *I*, can also be dropped
- the meaning changes to become more direct and may sound like an order delivered politely

> **3** Persuading by inviting – tʃəən-hâi เชิญ ให้
>
> I would like to invite him to go with us.
> ฉัน อยาก เชิญ ให้ เขา ไป ด้วย ค่ะ
> tʃán yàak *tʃəən-hâi-kháu* pai dûuai khâ
> I like *invite-make-he* go also khâ

- **tʃəən-hâi** เชิญ ให้ *to invite / to persuade*
- **hâi** ให้ can be used together with the verb **tʃəən-hâi** เชิญ ให้ *to invite*
- the polite ending particle **khâ** ค่ะ is used at the end to make the statement a bit softer

> **Short form**
> อยาก เชิญ ให้ เขา ไป ด้วย
> yàak *tʃəən-hâi-kháu* pai dûuai
> like *invite-make-he* go also

- when the meaning is understood from the context, the subject, here **tʃán** ฉัน *I,* can be dropped
- dropping the subject in Thai is quite common when speaking

> **B. Understanding hâi ให้ and persuading someone to do something**

- **hâi** ให้ and persuading
- **hâi** ให้ as a second element in the compound verb

Word order

Put **hâi** ให้ after the other verb in the sentence and before the object to whom the action is directed as follows:

Secret 12 – hâi ให้ with *persuasion* and *invitation*

> Subject + *tʃuuan-hâi-khun* + action verb
>
> I + *persuade-make-you* + stay = I persuade you to stay

The common verbs to urge someone to do something are:
- **tʃuuan-hâi** ชวน ให้ *to persuade*
- **khɔ̌ɔ-hâi** ขอ ให้ *to ask*
- **tʃəən-hâi** เชิญ ให้ *to invite* (very formal)

These verbs with **hâi** ให้ express different degrees of persuading. **tʃəən-hâi** *to invite* is used in formal situation only. **tʃuuan-hâi** ชวน ให้ *to persuade* is quite demanding. **khɔ̌ɔ-hâi** ขอ ให้ *to ask* can be used in many situations.

The invitation is made more polite by polite request particles such as:

nɔ̀i	หน่อย	*little*
dûuai	ด้วย	*also*
dâai-mǎi	ได้ไหม	*can you?*
khâ	ค่ะ	*polite particle for women*
khráp	ครับ	*polite particle for men*
ná	นะ	*ok?*

Strictly speaking, verbs like *to persuade, to ask, to invite* are not usually regarded as causative verbs in English. However, in Thai we may count them as causative verbs when used together with **hâi** ให้. *To persuade, to ask, to invite* can be used as a nice way to make someone else do something.

Conclusion

We may conclude that **hâi** ให้ is often used as a causative compound verb. It is usually placed before a pronoun, someone who needs to carry out the action. As a causative compound verb **hâi** ให้ points out the person whom the action is directed towards.

In this Secret, when **hâi** ให้ is used as a causative compound verb, its semantic boundaries are also defined by the other verb that it is used with.

The other verb together with **hâi** ให้ clarifies the meaning, such as **tʃuuan-hâi** ชวนให้ *to persuade*. The action verb, what type of action is in question, comes later in the sentence. The word order is Subject + *tʃuuan-hâi-khun* + action verb

The causative meaning of **hâi** ให้ is changed and softened by the use of polite ending particles.

Without *polite request particles* the persuasion would be too direct. Compare this Secret with Secret 6 *to request* and Secret 10 *to be polite*. The structure is the same. However, the words used are different, and consequently the meaning and the tone of the language are different.

C. Language hints

When **hâi** ให้ is used as the second element in a compound structure together with other verbs for *inviting* and *persuading*, the meaning is as follows:

1. To request by inviting

I would like to invite you to stay with me next week.
ฉัน อยาก เชิญ ให้ คุณ อยู่ กับ ฉัน อาทิตย์ หน้า นะ คะ
tʃán yàak *tʃəən-hâi-khun* yùu kàp tʃán aathít-nâa ná khá
I like want *invite-make-you* stay with I week next ná khá

Secret 12 – hâi ให้ with *persuasion* and *invitation*

- **tʃəən-hâi** เชิญ ให้ *to invite* is quite demanding since it is usually used as a formal request
- however, the person in question has a choice to accept the invitation, or he can also choose to do otherwise
- this structure is considered to be very formal

> **1.1** I invite you to stay with me next week.
> ฉัน เชิญ คุณ อยู่ กับ ฉัน อาทิตย์ หน้า นะ คะ
> tʃán *tʃəən-khun* yùu kàp tʃán aathít-nâa ná khá
> I like *invite-you* stay with I week next ná khá

- here **hâi** ให้ is dropped, and the main word **tʃəən** เชิญ is used alone without **hâi** ให้
- with some verbs, but not with all, **hâi** ให้ can be dropped. The rules for this are not exact. You need to learn them through using the language

> **2** To request by persuading
>
> I would like you to stay with me next week.
> ผม อยาก ชวน ให้ คุณ อยู่ กับ ผม อาทิตย์ หน้า ครับ
> phǒm yàak *tʃuuan-hâi-khun* yùu kàp phǒm aathít-nâa khráp
> I want *persuade-make-you* stay with I week next khráp

- **tʃuuan-hâi** ชวน ให้ *to persuade* is often used by Thais in speaking when wanting someone to do something
- in order to make wanting more polite, the polite request particles are used

3. To request by asking

I am asking you to stay with me next week.

ฉัน ขอ ให้ คุณ อยู่ กับ ฉัน อาทิตย์ หน้า นะ คะ
tʃán *khɔ̌ɔ-hâi-khun* yùu kàp tʃán aathít-nâa ná khá
I *ask-make-you* stay with I week next ná khá

- **khɔ̌ɔ-hâi** ขอ ให้ *to ask* is expressing a less demanding wish
- this sentence is somewhere between statements 1 and 2
- it is more than just an invitation, but less than strong persuasion

D. Simple advice

You may have already noticed that **khɔ̌ɔ-hâi** ขอ ให้ *to ask* is a very handy expression, which can be used in many different situations. Depending on the context and how it is said, it can express *wishing, polite asking, polite requesting, polite persuading* or even a *soft command* or *order*.

With ending one can change the emphasis. See more about **khɔ̌ɔ-hâi** ขอ ให้ in Secret 6 *to request* and Secret 11 *polite asking*

If you manage to add the following three words into your daily practice while communicating with Thai people, you are well on the way to understanding Thai people, their culture and language.

sànùk สนุก fun

- language and life should be "sànùk สนุก fun", otherwise Thai people would not feel very good

sàdùuak สะดวก convenient

- whatever is convenient and comfortable is right. There is no need to make simple things complicated

sàbaai สบาย to feel at ease

- to feel at ease and be happy is your birthright. Note that it is perfectly normal to smile at or with strangers in Thailand, as is not the case in many western countries

Perhaps one should add one more word:

sà-àat สะอาด to be clean and fresh

- to be and feel clean and fresh are very important personal qualities in Thailand

PART IV

hâi ให้ before pronouns, adjectives and adverbs

Part IV – hâi ให้ before pronouns, adjectives and adverbs

For him
ให้ เขา
hâi kháu

hâi is a very strong person, and she likes to help everybody. hâi says: "If my parents or friends have too much work, I can help them."

ให้ เป็น คน แข็ง แรง มาก – ให้ ชอบ ช่วย ทุกคน – ให้ บอก ว่า – ถ้า พ่อ แม่ หรือ เพื่อน มี งาน มาก เกินไป ฉัน ทำให้ได้ นะ คะ

hâi pen khon khěng-rɛɛng mâak – hâi tʃɔ̂ɔp tʃûuai thúk-khon – hâi bɔ̀ɔk-wâa – thâa phɔ̂ɔ-mɛ̂ɛ rǔɯ phɯ̂ɯan mii ngaan mâak gəən pai – tʃǎn tham-hâi dâai ná khá

hâi is person strong-strong very – hâi like help every person – hâi tell that – if father-mother or friend have work much over-go – I do-make can ná khá

SECRET 13

hâi ให้ as the preposition *for – for you... for me...*

In Thai **hâi** ให้ is strictly speaking a verb. In English, however, it can be best translated here as a preposition *for*. Many action verbs can be used in this way together with **hâi** ให้.

Secret 13 – hâi ให้ as the preposotion *for* – *for you... for me...*

A. Sentences

for him... for you... for everybody... and so on...

> **I**
>
> For him – hâi kháu ให้ เขา
>
> I wonder what I need to do for him.
>
> ฉัน สงสัย ว่า จะ ต้อง ทำ อะไร ให้ เขา
> tʃán sŏng-săi wâa tsà tôŋg tham arai *hâi-kháu*
> I wonder that will need do what *give-he*

- **hâi-kháu** ให้ เขา *for him*
- in Thai, the word **hâi** ให้ is a verb, and it really means *to give*. However, it is better translated here into English as the preposition *for*
- **hâi** ให้ is commonly placed before the pronoun meaning doing something *for* someone
- **hâi** ให้ is placed here before the pronoun **kháu** เขา *he*
- this structure is usually placed at the end of the sentence
- **hâi** ให้ is often used together with the verb **tham** ทำ *to do*

> **Short form**
>
> สงสัย ว่า จะ ต้อง ทำ อะไร ให้
> sŏng-săi wâa tsà tôŋg tham arai *hâi*
> wonder that will need do what *give*

- when the meaning is understood from the context, the subject **tʃán** ฉัน *I* and the object **kháu** เขา *he* can be dropped

Secret 13 – hâi ให้ as the preposotion *for* – *for you... for me...*

2 For you – hâi khun ให้ คุณ

I will do it for you.

ฉัน จะ ทำ ให้ คุณ
tʃán tsà tham *hâi-khun*
I will do *give-you*

- **hâi khun** ให้ คุณ *for you*
- in Thai the word **hâi** ให้ is a verb, and it really means *to give*. However, it is better translated here into English as the preposition *for*
- **hâi** ให้ here is placed before the pronoun **khun** คุณ *you*
- in this structure **hâi** ให้ is translated into English as *for*
- it is placed at the end of the sentence after the main verb

Short form

จะ ทำ ให้
tsà tham *hâi*
will do *give*

- when the meaning is understood from the context, the subject **tʃán** ฉัน *I* and the object **khun** คุณ *you* can be dropped

3 For everybody – hâi thúk-khon ให้ ทุก คน

I have enough work for everybody.

ฉัน มี งาน พอ จะ ให้ ทุก คน
tʃán mii ngaan phɔɔ tsà *hâi-thúk-khon*
I have work enough will *give-every-person*

- **hâi-thúk-khon** ให้ ทุก คน *for everybody*

- in Thai, the word **hâi** ให้ is a verb, and it really means *to give*. However, it is better translated here into English as the preposition *for*

- **hâi** ให้ here is placed before the pronoun **thúk-khon** ทุก คน *everybody*

> **Short form**
>
> มี งาน พอ ให้ ทุก คน
> mii ngaan phɔɔ *hâi-thúk-khon*
> have work enough *give-every-person*

- when the meaning is understood from the context the subject **tʃán** ฉัน *I* can be dropped

B. Understanding hâi ให้ as a preposition for

- **hâi** ให้ as *for you, for me*
- **hâi** ให้ as a preposition before a pronoun

Word order
Put **hâi** ให้ after the main verb and before the object, to whom the action is directed as follows:

> Subject + main verb + object + *hâi-thúk-khon*
>
> I + have + work + *give-everybody*
> = I have work for everybody

Here **hâi** ให้ is used as the preposition *for* as far as the English language is concerned.

However, in Thai the word **hâi** ให้ is a verb, and Thai people would perhaps understand **hâi** ให้ in this structure as *to give*.

In this structure **hâi** ให้ can be used together with many different action verbs.

Secret 13 – hâi ให้ as the preposotion *for* – *for you... for me...*

Example:

> I have enough work for everybody.
> ฉัน มี งาน พอ จะ ให้ ทุก คน
> tʃán mii ngaan phɔɔ tsà *hâi-thúk-khon*
> I have work enough will *give-every-person*

The above sentence could be translated more accurately into English as *I'll have enough work to give everybody* instead of *I have enough work for everybody.*

Note also that the helping verb **tsà** จะ *will*, which must always be followed by a verb, is placed before **hâi** ให้. This is just to illustrate the fact that the word **hâi** ให้ is a verb. It is most conveniently translated here into English as the preposition *for*

Conclusion

We may conclude that when the verb **hâi** ให้ comes after the main verb in the sentence, and when it is placed before the pronoun, it is usually translated into English as a preposition *for* or *to: for you, for me, to you, to me,* etc.

Even though **hâi** ให้ is a verb in Thai, we need to expand its semantic boundaries here to include the English prepositions *for* and *to*.

For Thai people **hâi** ให้ is one word, and the meaning is *to give*. However, its semantic boundary is much wider than the usage of the English word *to give*. Therefore, we need to use several different English words to grasp the correct meaning of **hâi** ให้. See more about the term "semantic boundary" and other grammar terms at the end of this book.

Secret 13 – hâi ให้ as the preposotion *for* – *for you... for me...*

The main verb, here **mii** มี *to have* is placed before the object, here **ngaan** งาน *work*.

The meaning is to do something or have something *for* someone, here **hâi-thúk-khon** ให้ ทุก คน *for everybody*.

Thai people understand the verb **hâi** ให้ intuitively usually from the context. The Thai way to understand the verb **hâi** ให้ here would be as *to give*.

C. Language hints

In Thai there are actually at least six or seven words, which can be translated into English as *for* or *to*. Their usage is somewhat different from each other depending on the circumstances. These expressions usually come at the end of the statement.

Examples:

To do something for someone: *for you, to you,* etc.

> **1**
>
> **hâi-khun** ให้ คุณ to you
>
> Who taught Thai to you?
>
> ใคร สอน ภาษา ไทย ให้ คุณ
> khrai sɔ̌ɔn phaasǎa-thai *hâi-khun*
> who teach language thai *give-you*

- **hâi** ให้ *to give* is translated here into English as *for* or *to*
- here **hâi** ให้ is placed before the pronoun, here **khun** คุณ *you*
- **hâi** ให้ is the verb that is commonly used in this kind of structure when speaking
- this statement can also be translated into English as *who taught you Thai?*

Secret 13 – hâi ให้ as the preposotion *for – for you... for me...*

> **2**
> fàak-khun ฝาก คุณ for you
> I bought vegetables for you.
> ฉัน ซื้อ ผัก มา ฝาก คุณ
> tʃán súu phàk maa *fàak-khun*
> I buy vegetable come *entrust-you*

- **fàak** ฝาก *to entrust, to deposit* used as a preposition *for, to*
- here **fàak** ฝาก meaning *for* or *to* is placed before the pronoun **khun** คุณ *you*
- **fàak** ฝาก is used in a way similar to **hâi** ให้
- in this context **fàak** ฝาก is understood more like as "giving a present"
- in Thai **fàak** ฝาก and **hâi** ให้ are verbs, but are better translated into English in sentences like those above as prepositions *for* or *to*

> **3**
> sămràp-khun สำหรับ คุณ for you
> This is for you.
> อัน นี้ สำหรับ คุณ
> an-níi *sămràp-khun*
> piece-this *for-you*

- **sămràp** สำหรับ is a somewhat more formal way to express meanings like *for* or *to*
- here **sămràp** สำหรับ *for, to* is placed before the pronoun **khun** คุณ *you*
- **sămràp** สำหรับ *for, to* is used in a way similar to **hâi** ให้
- however, **sămràp** สำหรับ *for* is a preposition and **hâi** ให้ is a verb

Secret 13 – hâi ให้ as the preposotion *for – for you... for me...*

4 sùuan-tʃán ส่วน ฉัน – as for me, to me

For me, it is too cold here.

ส่วน ฉัน ที่นี่ หนาว เกินไป
sùuan tʃán thîi-nîi năau kəən-pai
for I place-this cold beyond-go

- here **sùuan** ส่วน *for* is placed before the pronoun **tʃán** ฉัน *me*. It is used as an introduction to the subject as the English phrase "as for me"
- in this context **sùuan** ส่วน *for* is placed at the beginning of the sentence

5 phûua-khun เพื่อ คุณ for you

I will do everything for you. (for your sake)

ผม จะ ทำ ทุก อย่าง เพื่อ คุณ
phŏm tsà tham thúk-yàang phûua-khun
I will do what *for-you*

- here **phûua** เพื่อ *for, to* is placed before the pronoun **khun** คุณ *you*
- **phûua** เพื่อ *for, to* is used in the similar way as **hâi** ให้ *for, to*
- however, the meaning differs. The preposition **phûua** เพื่อ here means, *for your sake: I will do anything for your sake*

6 kàp / kɛ̀ɛ khun กับ / แก่ คุณ to you

I'll give red roses to you.

ผม ให้ ดอก กุหลาบ สี แดง กับ คุณ
phŏm hâi-dɔ̀ɔk-gùlàap sĭi dɛɛng kàp-khun
I give-flower-rose colour red *with-you*

Secret 13 – hâi ให้ as the preposotion *for – for you... for me...*

- this statement is grammatically different since **hâi** ให้ is used here as a main verb *to give*
- here we have two choices, we can use either **kàp** กับ *with* or **kὲε** แก่ *to*. The latter is more formal and is seldom used in speaking
- **hâi** ให้ as *a main verb* before a noun means *to give* something to someone
- **hâi** ให้ as a main verb is placed before a noun, here **dɔ̀ɔk-gùlàap** ดอกกุหลาบ *rose* followed by to whom the object is given
- see more about **hâi** ให้ *to give* in Secrets 1 and 2

D. Simple advice

In order to become fluent in Thai you need a lot of practice. Listen to the audio CD's read by native Thai speakers, again and again. Repeat sentences aloud yourself again and again until you are able to speak intuitively. If you do not understand something, then read the grammatical explanation. When learning a second language like Thai, you need practice, repetition and also perhaps some skill with grammar.

Listening regularly to Thai will help attune your ear to the language and aid your understanding of what you hear. Understanding grammar will help you to form correct sentences. It is also important to break the habit of forcing the structure of your own language onto Thai. You need to be active in your language use, seeking to use the language in many different ways.

Note also that how to produce sounds is very important in Thai. Be aware that learning the Thai script does not help you to understand Thai sounds any better. Sounds are sounds, and it does not matter how they are written. You need to learn every sound first, one by one, and then how they are written in Thai.

If in doubt, please read the book *22 Secrets of Learning Thai – Complete Guide to Sounds, Tones and Thai writing System*. Then practise and adjust your speaking until you can make new sounds correctly. By knowing how new sounds are made both in theory and practice, you will become more confident in learning Thai.

Secret 14 – hâi ให้ before adjectives

Write *beautifully!*
เขียน ให้ สวย
khĭian *hâi-sŭuai*

---

hâi likes to behave nicely. hâi says: "Dress beautifully, do everything well and do not forget to finish important work."

ให้ ชอบ ทำ ตัว ให้ สวย – ให้ บอก ว่า – แต่ง ตัว ให้ สวย – ทำ ทุก สิ่ง ทุก อย่าง ให้ ดี – อย่า ลืม ทำ งาน ที่ สำคัญ ให้ เสร็จ

hâi tɟɔ̌ɔp tham-tuua hâi-sŭuai – hâi bɔ̀ɔk-wâa – tɛ̀ɛng-tuua hâi-sŭuai – tham thúk-sìng thúk-yàang hâi-dii – yàa lɯɯm tham ngaan thîi sămkhan hâi-sèt

hâi like do-body make-beautiful – hâi tell that – prepare-body make-beautiful do every-thing every-kind make-good – no forget do work that important make-finish

Secret 14

hâi ให้ before an adjective expresses *a command*

hâi ให้ is often used to turn an adjective into an adverb. Before an adjective **hâi** ให้ conveys some sort of wish, demand or command as for example:

khǐian hâi-sǔuai
เขียน ให้ สวย
write beautifully

Secret 14 – hâi ให้ before adjectives

A. Sentences

hâi before adjectives is a command

> **1** Beautifully – hâi-sŭuai เขียน ให้ สวย
> Would you write beautifully!
> เขียน ให้ สวย ได้ ไหม
> khĭian *hâi-sŭuai* dâai-mái
> write *make-beautiful* can-question!

- khĭian **hâi-sŭuai** เขียน ให้ สวย *Write beautifully!*
- **hâi** ให้ before an adjective turns an adjective into an adverb
- the verb **khĭian** เขียน *to write* + **hâi** ให้ + an adjective **sŭuai** สวย *beautiful* is expressing the command how one should behave, *to write beautifully!*
- **dâai-mái** ได้ ไหม at the end of the sentence softens the command

> **Short form**
> เขียน ให้ สวย
> khĭian *hâi-sŭuai*
> write *make-beautiful*

- khĭian **hâi-sŭuai** เขียน ให้ สวย *Write beautifully!*
- when **dâai-mái** ได้ ไหม, a polite question particle, is dropped the colour of the statement changes
- this structure is more direct, more of a command or an instruction than the previous sentence

Secret 14 – hâi ให้ before adjectives

2. Nicely – hâi-dii ให้ ดี
Please try to behave nicely.
ช่วย พยายาม ทำ ตัว ให้ ดี
tʃûuai pháyaayaam tham-tuua *hâi-dii*
please try do-body *make-good*

- **tham-tuua hâi-dii** ทำตัว ให้ ดี *Behave nicely!*
- **hâi** ให้ before an adjective turns an adjective into an adverb
- the verb **tham-tuua** ทำ ตัว *to behave* + **hâi** ให้ + an adjective **dii** ดี *good* is expressing an instruction as to how one should behave, *nicely, well*
- **tʃûuai** ช่วย *please* at the beginning of the sentence softens the command

Short form
ทำ ตัว ให้ ดี
tham-tuua *hâi-dii*
do-body *make-good*

- **tham-tuua hâi-dii** ทำตัว ให้ ดี *Behave nicely!*
- when the word **tʃûuai** ช่วย *please* is dropped the colour of the statement changes
- this structure is more of a direct command. It is much stronger than the instruction of the previous sentence

3. Correctly – hâi-thùuk-tɔ̂ng ให้ ถูก ต้อง
He must guess it correctly.
เขา ต้อง ทาย ให้ ถูก ต้อง
kháu tɔ̂ng thaai *hâi-thùuk-tɔ̂ng*
he must guess *make-correct-must*

- **thaai hâi-thùuk-tông** ทาย ให้ ถูก ต้อง *Guess correctly!*
- the verb **thaai** ทาย *to guess* + **hâi** ให้ + an adjective **thùuk-tông** ถูก ต้อง *correct* is expressing the command how one should behave, *to guess correctly*

> **Short form**
>
> ต้อง ทาย ให้ ถูก ต้อง
> tông thaai *hâi-thùuk-tông*
> must guess *make-correct-must*

- **thaai hâi-thùuk-tông** ทาย ให้ ถูก ต้อง *Guess correctly!*
- when the context is clear, the subject **kháu** เขา can be dropped as it is common in speaking

B. Understanding hâi ให้ before adjectives

- **hâi** ให้ + an adjective denotes a command
- **hâi** ให้ is placed after the main verb and before an adjective

Word order
Put **hâi** ให้ after the action verb and before an adjective as follows:

> Commanding verb + *hâi-sŭuai*
>
> write + *make-beautiful* = write beautifully!

When **hâi** ให้ is put before an adjective, it converts an adjective into an adverb.

hâi ให้ + adjective describes the fact how and in what way the action should be happening. This structure also tells somebody the way one should behave. The sentence denotes some sort of wish, demand or command. It is an imperative structure.

Consider the following sentences:

Secret 14 – hâi ให้ before adjectives

1 Walk beautifully!
เดิน ให้ สวย
dəən *hâi-sŭuai*
walk *make-beautiful*

- verb + **hâi** ให้ + adjective expresses a command. This structure is telling someone how they should walk, *beautifully!*

2 I'll have to drive carefully.
ผม จะ ขับ ให้ ดี
phŏm tsà khàp *hâi-dii*
I will drive *make-good*

- here verb + **hâi** ให้ + adjective is not a command
- it is however an imperative structure expressing promise or intension
- when **hâi** ให้ is directed towards the speaker and placed before an adjective, it can be translated into English as *a must* to do something in that way

Conclusion

When **hâi** ให้ is placed before an *adjective*, it turns an adjective into an adverb. This usually happens when the structure is a command. The subject wants someone else to behave or carry out the action in a certain way.

Even though **hâi** ให้ is a verb in Thai, we need to expand its semantic boundaries here to include English adverbs of manner. With **hâi** ให้ the adjective *beautiful* changes to an adverb *beautifully*.

However, Thai people understand the verb **hâi** ให้ intuitively usually from the context. The Thai way to understand the verb **hâi** ให้ here would be as *to make*. Yet, if you ask the Thai people what the word **hâi** ให้ means here, they will most like say that it means to *give*.

C. Language hints

a) There are many more ways to make adjectives become adverbs. Consider the following sentences:

1
She can walk beautifully.
เขา เดิน ได้ สวย
kháu dəən *dâai-sŭuai*
she walk *can-beatiful*

- **dâai** ได้ + adjective describes the fact how well somebody can do something

- this structure is not a command. It is describing the fact that she walks beautifully

Secret 14 – hâi ให้ before adjectives

> **2**
> She walks beautifully.
> เขา เดิน สวย
> kháu dəən *sǔuai*
> she walk *beatiful*

- when speaking, the short form is often preferred without **dâai** ได้
- this sentence describes how or in what way the action is happening

> **3**
> She walks beautifully.
> เขา เดิน อย่าง สวย
> kháu dəən *yàang-sǔuai*
> she walk *manner-beautiful*

- **yàang** อย่าง + adjective describes how or in what way the action is happening
- this structure is not a command. It describes the manner how she walks

b) The following is a short reminder how to use classifiers in Thai.

Examples:

> **1**
> She is beautiful.
> เขา สวย
> kháu sǔuai
> she beautiful

- adjectives in Thai can play the role of both a verb and an adjective in the sentence.

Secret 14 – hâi ให้ before adjectives

2.
She is beautiful.
เขา เป็น คน สวย
kháu *pen-khon* sŭuai
she *be-person* beautiful

- if you use the verb **pen** เป็น *to be*, a classifier is needed, here **khon** คน *person*

3. *Warning*
It is not correct Thai to say:
She is beautiful.
เขา เป็น สวย
kháu *pen* sŭuai
she *be* beautiful

- if you did speak like that, you would be understood but regarded as speaking broken Thai

D. Simple advice

Every word in Thai has usually a specific meaning. Here we would like to demonstrate how the meaning changes when we add the verb **hâi** ให้ into the simple basic sentence. Consider the following sentences:

1.
Subject + verb + adjective
He walks beautifully.
เขา เดิน สวย
kháu dəən *sŭuai*
he walk *beautiful*

- action verb + adjective = an adverb, *beautifully*
- the verb + adjective without **hâi** ให้ is expressing how he walks

- this structure is telling how she walks, *beautifully!*
- without **hâi** ให้ the statement is descriptive and conveys no command

> **2**
>
> Subject + verb + **hâi** ให้ + adjective
>
> He must walk beautifully.
>
> เขา ต้อง เดิน ให้ สวย
> kháu tông dəən *hâi-sŭuai*
> he must walk *make-beautiful*

- **hâi** ให้ + adjective = an adverb, *must walk beautifully*
- this is an *imperative structure*
- with **hâi** ให้ the sentence is stronger
- here the statement expresses the fact how he should behave, it is a must

> **3**
>
> verb + **hâi** ให้ + adjective
>
> Walk beautifully.
>
> เดิน ให้ สวย
> dəən *hâi-sŭuai*
> walk *make-beautiful*

- verb + **hâi** ให้ + adjective = *make* or *do it beautifully*
- this structure is a *direct command*
- when we start the sentence with the action verb, this kind of structure with **hâi** ให้ transforms the statement into a direct command
- when expressing commands **hâi** ให้ is usually placed before the adjective and cannot be dropped

Secret 15 – hâi ให้ before adverbs

Far away!
ให้ไกล
hâi-glai

hâi is a curious person. hâi says: "Sometimes I like to disappear and go somewhere. There are many things I want to see."

ให้ เป็น คน ที่ อยาก รู้ อยาก เห็น – ให้ บอก ว่า – บาง ครั้ง ฉัน ชอบ หาย ตัว แล้ว ก็ ไป ให้ ทั่ว – มี หลาย สิ่ง เยอะ แยะ ที่ ฉัน อยาก จะ เห็น

hâi pen khon thîi yàak-rúu yàak-hěn – hâi bɔ̀ɔk-wâa – baang-khráng tʃán tʃɔ̂ɔp hǎai-tuua lɛ́ɛu gɔ̂ɔ pai hâi-thûua – mii lǎai sìng yá-yɛ́ thîi tʃán yàak tsà hěn

hâi be person that want-know want-see – hâi tell that – some-time I like disappear-body then also go make-everywhere – have many thing much-much that I want will see

Secret 15

hâi ให้ before adverbs tells us more about the action

hâi ให้ is also used directly with adverbs to tell more about the action in question, as for example:

khón hâi-thûua
ค้น ให้ ทั่ว
seek everywhere

or

yùu hâi-naan-naan
อยู่ ให้ นาน-นาน
to stay a very long time

Secret 15 – hâi ให้ before adverbs

A. Sentences

hâi ให้ before an adverb tells more about the action in question

1 Far away – hâi-glai ให้ ไกล
I will walk far.
ฉัน จะ เดิน ไป ให้ ไกล
tʃán tsà dəən pai *hâi-glai*
I will walk go *make-far*

- **pai hâi-glai** ให้ ไกล *to walk far away*
- here **hâi** ให้ is placed directly before the adverb **glai** ไกล *far*
- this sentence is not a command
- it tells us more about the action in question

Short form
จะ เดิน ให้ ไกล
tsà dəən *hâi-glai*
will walk *make-far*

- when the meaning is understood from the context, the subject **tʃán** ฉัน *I* can be dropped

2 Everywhere, all over – hâi-thûua ให้ ทั่ว
I will go everywhere.
ฉัน จะ ไป ให้ ทั่ว
tʃán tsà pai *hâi-thûua*
I will go *make-everywhere*

- **pai hâi-thûua** ไป ให้ ทั่ว *to go everywhere*
- here **hâi** ให้ is placed directly before the adverb **thûua** ทั่ว *everywhere*

Secret 15 – hâi ให้ before adverbs

- this statement is not a command
- it tells us more about the action in question

> **Short form**
>
> จะ ไป ให้ ทั่ว
> tsà pai *hâi-thûua*
> will go *make-everywhere*

- when the meaning is understood from the context, the subject **tʃán** ฉัน *I* can be dropped

3 Very long time – hâi-naan-naan ให้ นานๆ

I will stay a very long time.

ฉัน จะ อยู่ ให้ นานๆ
tʃán tsà yùu *hâi-naan-naan*
I will stay *make-long-long*

- **yùu hâi-naan-naan** อยู่ ให้ นานๆ *to stay very long time*
- here **hâi** ให้ is placed directly before the adverb **naan-naan** นานๆ *very long time*
- this statement is not a command
- it tells us more about the action in question

> **Short form**
>
> จะ อยู่ ให้ นานๆ
> tsà yùu hâi-naan-naan
> will stay *make-long-long*

- when the meaning is understood from the context, the subject **tʃán** ฉัน *I* can be dropped

B. Understanding hâi ให้ before adverbs

- **hâi** ให้ + an adverb tells more about the action
- **hâi** ให้ is placed after the main verb and before an adverb

Word order

Put **hâi** ให้ before the adverb as follows:

> Subject + main verb + *hâi-glai*
>
> I + walk + *make-far* = I walk far

hâi ให้ is used directly with an adverb to tell us more about the intended action. I'll do it that way.

hâi ให้ before an adverb emphasises the manner in which the action is performed.

The statement can be turned into a command by starting the sentence with the command verb as follows:

> Command verb + *hâi-glai*
>
> walk + *make-far* = walk far

Note that the word **hâi** ให้ is a verb in Thai. It is not always very easy to give a direct translation into English. Perhaps the closest we can come here is to translate it as *to make*.

In similar cases English uses only an *adverb*, here *far*.

Conclusion

hâi ให้ can be placed directly before an adverb in order to tell us more about the action. This structure can be *descriptive* or *a command*.

Even though **hâi** ให้ is a verb in Thai, we need to expand its semantic boundaries to include English adverbs.

Secret 15 – hâi ให้ before adverbs

Example:

> **tsà yùu hâi-naan-naan**
> จะ อยู่ ให้ นานๆ
> I'll stay for a very long time

These kinds of statements usually convey the idea that *I'll do it that way.*

However, Thai people understand the verb **hâi** ให้ intuitively usually from the context. The Thai way to understand the verb **hâi** ให้ here would be *to make* or more literally *to give.*

On the other hand, **hâi** ให้ + adjective is usually a *command.* It describes how and in what way the action should be happening. See the previous Secret 14.

C. Language hints

Just to remind you of the fact that **hâi** ให้ can be put before nouns, pronouns, adjectives and adverbs to express different meanings.

Examples:

> **1** hâi ให้ as a main verb before nouns = *to give*
>
> I give a pen to you.
> ฉัน ให้ ปากกา คุณ
> tʃán *hâi-pàak-kaa* khun
> I *give-pen* you

- as a main verb and before a noun in the sentence, **hâi** ให้ is translated into English as *to give*

Secret 15 – hâi ให้ before adverbs

2 hâi ให้ as a causative verb before the pronoun = *to let, to request, to order*

I let him stay here.

ผม ให้ เขา อยู่ ที่ นี่
phŏm *hâi-kháu* yùu thîi-nîi
I *let he* stay place-this

- before a pronoun **hâi** ให้ is translated here into English as *to let, to make* or even *to order* depending on the context

3 hâi ให้ before adjectives = command

Drive properly.

ขับ ให้ ดี
khàp *hâi-dii*
drive *make-good*

- often before an adjective **hâi** ให้ is used like an adverb in English when *giving commands*

3.1 hâi ให้ before adjectives = must, have to

I'll have to drive carefully.

ผม จะ ขับ ให้ ดี
phŏm tsà khàp *hâi-dii*
I will drive *make-good*

- here **hâi** ให้ is not a command
- when **hâi** ให้ is directed towards the speaker and placed before an adjective, it can be translated into English as *must* do something in that way

Secret 15 – hâi ให้ before adverbs

4 hâi ให้ before an adverb = tells us more about the action

I must come to work regularly.
ฉัน ต้อง มา ทำ งาน ให้ สม่ำเสมอ
tʃǎn tôŋg maa tham-ngaan *hâi-sàmàm-sàmǒə*
I must come do-work *make-regular*

- before an adverb in the sentence, **hâi** ให้ is translated into English as to tell more about the action in question
- this statement is descriptive and imperative
- it is directed towards the speaker

4.1 Stay for a very long time!
อยู่ ให้ นานๆ
yùu hâi-naan-naan
stay *make-long-long*

- **yùu hâi-naan-naan** อยู่ ให้ นาน นาน *stay for a very long time*
- here **hâi** ให้ is placed directly before the adverb **naan-naan** นานๆ *very long time*
- this statement is a suggestion or a mild request for someone to stay *for a very long time*
- it is directed towards the other person
- it tells us more about the action in question and how it should happen

> **5** hâi ให้ after the main verb and before a pronoun as *for you, for me...*
>
> I made some food for you.
> ฉัน ทำ อาหาร ให้ คุณ
> tʃán tham aahăan *hâi-khun*
> I do food *give-you*

- here **hâi** ให้ is placed after the main verb, **tham** ทำ *to do* and before the pronoun **khun** คุณ *you*
- in English **hâi** ให้ is best translated in this type of structure as *for*
- however, the word **hâi** ให้ is a verb, and Thais would perhaps understand it here as *to give*

D. Simple advice

> Regarding *transliterations* in Thai, you probably know already that there is no one way to *transliterate* Thai sounds using western letters of the alphabet. This can be confusing since every book seems to have a slightly different way to transliterate similar sounds.

The Royal Thai system is the only official transliteration system in use. It is mainly used for proper names and road signs in Thailand. However, it has several shortcomings when describing Thai sounds accurately. For instance, it does not differentiate between short and long vowels, and it usually omits the tone marks. It is therefore not often used in language schools or in Thai learning books.

Vowels are very important components in the Thai language – more important than they are in English. English has only five vowel letters while Thai has more than 18. The Thai language is vowel-oriented in the sense that vowels and vowel combinations play a very important part in the spoken language. Vowels in Thai must be pronounced clearly short or long. Thai is a tonal language and its five different tones are placed on the vowel sound.

English on the other hand relies more on consonant sounds, and there is no need to pronounce all vowel sounds clearly in order to be understood. In the beginning, we would advise the Thai language learner to focus attention on the vowel qualities in spoken Thai.

In English, vowels are pronounced with great variety by different groups of English speaking people. Yet, there is not much difficulty in understanding different accents. In Thai, vowels are more clear and precise. They cannot be blurred into *schwa* or changed into something else if you want to be easily understood by Thais.

Until arriving...
ให้ ถึง
hâi thǔng

hâi is also patient. hâi says: "Sometimes we need to be patient. There is no need to do anything. For example, it is better to wait until the fruit is ripe before eating it."

ให้ มี ความ อดทน ด้วย – ให้ บอก ว่า – บาง ครั้ง เรา ต้อง มี ความ อดทน – ไม่ ต้อง ทำ อะไร เลย – ตัว อย่าง เช่น คอย ผลไม้ ให้ สุก ก่อน จะ กิน ดีกว่า

hâi mii khwaam-òtthon dûuai – hâi bɔ̀ɔk-wâa – baang-khráng rau tông mii khwaam-òtthon – mâi tông tham arai lə̌əi – tuua-yàang chên khɔɔi phǒn-lá-máai hâi-sùk kɔ̀ɔn tsà kin dii-gwàa

hâi have matter-tolerance also – hâi tell that – sometime we must have matter-tolerance – no must do what excess – character-sort as wait fruit-plant let-ripe before will eat good-more

SECRET 16

hâi ให้ as *until*

hâi ให้ can be used meaning *until*, as in for example **khɔɔi-hâi pŏm...** คอย ให้ ผม *Wait for me until...* Even in Thai **hâi** ให้ is strictly speaking a verb, but here in English it can be best translated as the conjunction *until*. It is often understood as a kind of wish or command.

Secret 16 – hâi ให้ as *until*

A. Sentences

hâi ให้ as *until*

> **1** Until coming – hâi thǔng ให้ ถึง
>
> Walk until you come to the temple.
>
> เดิน ไป ให้ ถึง วัด
> dəən-pai *hâi-thǔng-wát*
> walk-go *let-arrive-temple*

- **hâi-thǔng-wát** ให้ ถึง วัด *until coming to the temple or until arriving to the temple*
- **hâi** ให้ is placed before the verb, here **thǔng** ถึง *to arrive*
- **hâi** ให้ as *until* is usually used in connection with commands and when giving directions or orders
- place **hâi** ให้ after the verb that expresses the command, here **dəən-pai** เดิน ไป *to walk* and before the verb, here **thǔng** ถึง *to arrive, to reach*
- **hâi** ให้ is understood here as *to let*
- however, in this context **hâi** ให้ is best translated into English as the conjunction *until*

> **Short form**
>
> เดิน ไป ถึง วัด
> dəən-pai *thǔng-wát*
> walk-go *arrive-temple*

- **thǔng-wát** ถึง วัด *until coming to temple*
- the short form is often used in spoken Thai without **hâi** ให้ while giving instructions or suggestions
- however, with **hâi** ให้ the statement is stronger

Secret 16 – hâi ให้ as *until*

2 Wait until... – khɔɔi hâi... คอย ให้...

Wait for me until I come.

คอย ให้ ฉัน มา
khɔɔi *hâi-tʃán-maa*
wait *let-I-come*

- **hâi-tʃán-maa** ให้ ฉัน มา *until I come*
- place **hâi** ให้ after the verb that expresses the command, here **khɔɔi** คอย *to wait* and before the pronoun, here **tʃán** ฉัน *I*
- **hâi** ให้ is understood here as *to let*
- however, in this context **hâi** ให้ is best translated into English as the conjunction *until*

Short form

คอย ฉัน มา
khɔɔi *tʃán-maa*
wait *I-come*

- **tʃán-maa** ฉัน มา *until I come*
- the short form without **hâi** ให้ is often preferred in spoken language
- this sentence is not as strong as the complete statement with **hâi** ให้

3 Until full – hâi tem ให้ เต็ม

Please fill the tank with gasoline until it is full.

เติม น้ำ มัน ให้ เต็ม ถัง ค่ะ
təəm náam-man *hâi-tem-thăng* khâ
fill water-oil *let-full-tank* please

- **hâi-tem-thăng** ให้ เต็ม ถัง *until full tank*
- **hâi** ให้ is placed before the adverb, here **tem** เต็ม *full*
- place **hâi** ให้ after the verb that expresses the command, here **tɔɔm** เติม *to add* and before the adverb **tem** เต็ม *full*
- **hâi** ให้ is understood here as *to let*
- however, in this context **hâi** ให้ is best translated into English as a conjunction *until*

Short form

เติม น้ำ มัน เต็ม ถัง ค่ะ
tɔɔm náam-man *tem* thăng khâ
fill water-oil *full* tank please

- **tem-thăng** เต็ม ถัง *until full tank*
- the short form without **hâi** ให้ is often preferred when speaking
- however, with **hâi** ให้ the statement is stronger

B. Understanding hâi ให้ as until

- **hâi** ให้ meaning *until*
- **hâi** ให้ as *until* can be placed before *nouns, pronouns* or *verbs*

Word order
Put **hâi** ให้ after the main verb as follows:

verb + *hâi-tʃán-maa*

wait + *let-I-come* = wait for me until I come

hâi ให้ meaning *until* in the sentence is often used when giving directions and commands.

In English **hâi ให้** is best translated here as a conjunction *until*. Note, however, that the word **hâi ให้** is a verb.

hâi ให้ can also be understood here as *to let*. This is one of those cases where the two languages, Thai and English, use different parts of speech in order to express the same meaning. In this case, Thai uses the verb **hâi ให้** *to let* while English uses the conjunction *until*.

In the short form without **hâi ให้**, we would still use the conjunction *until* in the English translation.

In Thai, there are many other ways to express the English word *until*. See language hints in this Secret.

Conclusion

hâi ให้ can be placed after a command verb followed by pronouns, verbs, adverbs and also adjectives. The translation into English in this structure is usually *until*.

Even though **hâi ให้** is a verb in Thai, we need to expand its semantic boundaries here to include the English conjunction word *until*.

However, Thai people understand the verb **hâi ให้** intuitively usually from the context. The Thai way to understand the verb **hâi ให้** here would be *to let*.

C. Language hints

There are also other ways to express *until* as follows:

1 tson จน

He ate until he was full.

เขา กิน ข้าว จน อิ่ม
kháu kin khâau *tson* ìm
he eat rice *until* full

2 thŭng ถึง

I shall stay here until next year.

ผม จะ อยู่ ที่ นี่ ถึง ปี หน้า
phŏm tsà yùu thîi-nîi *thŭng* pii-nâa
I shall stay place-this *reach* year-next

3 tson-thŭng จน ถึง

Wait until Songkran.

คอย จน ถึง สงกรานต์
khɔɔi *tson-thŭng* sŏng-kraan
wait *until-reach* Songkran

4 tson-gwàa จน กว่า

We shall wait until he comes.

เรา จะ รอ จน กว่า เขา จะ มา
rao tsà rɔɔ *tson-gwàa* kháu tsà maa
we shall wait *until-more* he will come

Secret 16 – hâi ให้ as *until*

D. Simple advice

Translating from one language to another is not always easy. It is only natural that you try unconsciously or consciously to impose the structure of your own language into Thai.

But if you are able to think as Thai people do when using the verb **hâi** ให้, you may learn Thai faster and will be able to choose the right word in the relevant situation.

Example:

> Wait until I come.
> คอย ให้ ฉัน มา
> khɔɔi *hâi tʃǎn* maa
> wait *let I* come

This is one of those examples when the English language uses a different grammatical stucture in the translation of the verb **hâi** ให้. The correct translation of this sentence into English is *Wait until I come*.

However, the word **hâi** ให้ is a verb, and the Thai way to think about this statement is *Wait let me come*. If you understand how Thai people think and use the verb **hâi** ให้ in this situation, then it would perhaps be easier for you to express yourself correctly in Thai.

Secret 17 – hâi ให้ in idiomatic expressions

Go away, leave me alone!
ไป ให้ พ้น ดี กว่า
pai-hâi-phón

> hâi is a very special person. hâi says: "My name is hâi, and I am not afraid of anything. That's the way I am."
>
> ให้ เป็น คน พิเศษ มาก – ให้ บอก ว่า – ฉัน ชื่อ ให้ – ฉัน ไม่ กลัว ไม่ ว่า จะ เกิด อะไร ขึ้น – ฉัน ก็ จะ เป็น แบบ นี้
>
> hâi pen khon phísèet mâak – hâi bɔ̀ɔk-wâa – tʃǎn tʃɯ̂ɯ hâi – tʃǎn mâi gluua mâi wâa tsà gə̀ət-arai-kɯ̂n – tʃǎn kɔ̂ɔ tsà pen bɛ̀ɛp-níi
>
> hâi is person special very – hâi tell that – I name hâi – I no afraid no that will happen-what-rise – I then will be style-this

Secret 17

hâi ให้ in special idiomatic expressions

hâi ให้ is often used in special expressions in certain idiomatic ways that cannot always be translated directly into English.

Good examples are **hâi** ให้ as in:

pai-hâi-phón	ไป ให้ พ้น	*leave me alone!*
hâi-dâai	ให้ ได้	*whatever happens!*
hâi-pen-pai	ให้ เป็นไป	*let it be!*

Secret 17 – hâi ให้ in idiomatic expressions

A. Sentences

hâi in idiomatic expressions

> **1**
>
> Leave me alone! – pai-hâi-phón ไป ให้ พ้น
>
> It would be better you leave me alone!
>
> ไป ให้ พ้น ดี กว่า
> *pai-hâi-phón* dii gwàa
> *go-let-beyond* good more

- **pai-hâi-phón** ไป ให้ พ้น *Leave me alone! Go away!*
- here **hâi** ให้ is placed between the verb **pai** ไป *to go* and verb **phón** พ้น *to pass, to go beyond*
- this expression is usually translated into English as *Leave me alone! / Go away!*

> **Short form**
>
> ไป ให้ พ้น
> *pai-hâi-phón*
> *go-let-beyond*

- **pai-hâi-phón** ไป ให้ พ้น *Leave me alone! Go away!*
- the simple short form is often preferred in spoken language
- however, with **dii-gwàa** ดี กว่า the statement is softer

> **2**
>
> Whatever happens! – hâi-dâai ให้ ได้
>
> I will go whatever happens.
>
> ฉัน จะ ไป ให้ ได้
> tʃán tsà pai *hâi-dâai*
> I will go *let-can*

Secret 17 – hâi ให้ in idiomatic expressions

- **hâi-dâai** ให้ได้ *Whatever happens!*
- here **hâi** ให้ is placed before the verb **dâai** ได้ *to get*
- it is usually translated into English as *whatever happens, in any case*

Short form

จะ ไป ให้ ได้
tsà pai *hâi-dâai*
will go *let-can*

- **hâi-dâai** ให้ได้ *Whatever happens!*
- the subject **tʃán** ฉัน *I* is usually left out in spoken language

3

Let it be! – hâi-pen-pai ให้ เป็น ไป

Leave it! Let it be!

ปล่อย ให้ มัน เป็น ไป
plɔ̀ɔi *hâi-man-pen-pai*
release *let-it-be-go*

- **plɔ̀ɔi-hâi-pen-pai** ปล่อย ให้ เป็น ไป *Let it be!*
- here **hâi** ให้ is placed before the object **man** มัน *it* followed by **pen-pai** เป็น ไป *be-go*
- the statement is usually translated into English as *Let it be! / Forget it!*

Short form

ให้ มัน เป็น ไป
hâi-man-pen-pai
let-it-be-go

- **hâi-pen-pai** ปล่อย ให้ เป็น ไป *Let it be!*

- the verb **plòi** ปล่อย *to release* can be dropped without changing the meaning

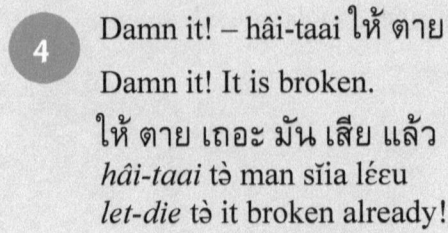

Damn it! – hâi-taai ให้ ตาย

Damn it! It is broken.

ให้ ตาย เถอะ มัน เสีย แล้ว
hâi-taai tə̀ man sǐia lέεu
let-die tə̀ it broken already!

- **hâi-taai** ให้ ตาย *Damn it!*
- here **hâi** ให้ is placed before the verb **taai** ตาย *to die*
- this statement is often translated into English as *Damn it! / My goodness!*
- **tə̀** เถอะ here is not translated. It just gives more emphasis to the statement
- the word **tə̀** เถอะ is also often used with the expression **pai kan-tə̀** ไป กัน เถอะ *Let's go!*

Short form

ให้ ตาย เถอะ
hâi-taai tə̀
make-die tə̀

- **hâi-taai** ให้ ตาย *Damn it! / My goodness!*
- the last part of the sentence can be left out if the meaning is understood from the context

B. Understanding hâi ให้ in idiomatic expressions

- **hâi** ให้ and special idiomatic expressions
- **hâi** ให้ plays a central role in many idiomatic expressions in Thai

Word order

Put **hâi** ให้ in idiomatic expressions as follows:

verb + hâi + verb

go-let-beyond = Go away! Leave me alone!

The exact semantic boundaries of **hâi** ให้ don't always match directly with the English language. This is often so in idiomatic expressions. The meaning here is understood from context as is often the case in Thai.

hâi ให้ is understood here as *to make* or *to let*. However, the correct meaning of **hâi** ให้ usually hints at some sort of command and getting someone to do something. At other times in idiomatic expressions the meaning may express frustration, unhappiness or surprise over a matter.

> **Conclusion**
>
> Sometimes **hâi** ให้ seems not to have any exact meaning by itself. However, if we leave the verb **hâi** ให้ out, the meaning of the statement changes or is not complete.
>
> To translate subtle nuances of the verb **hâi** ให้ into English, when **hâi** ให้ is used together with other words in different contexts, is not always possible. We may need to use totally different English words and structures in order to get the meaning across.

C. Language hints

Idiomatic expressions are used in a special way, and they need to be learned by heart. There are no straightforward rules on how to translate them.

Usually however, there are simple rules about how **hâi** ให้ is used in a sentence.

Secret 17 – hâi ให้ in idiomatic expressions

Examples:

① hâi ให้ as a main verb *to give*

I will give you a watch.

ฉัน จะ ให้ นาฬิกา คุณ
tʃán *hâi-naalikaa* khun
I *give-watch* you

- here **hâi** ให้ as a main verb alone before the noun **naalikaa** นาฬิกา *watch* is translated into English as *to give*

② hâi ให้ as a causative verb *to let, to request, to order*

He made me come.

เขา ให้ ผม มา
kău *hâi-pŏm* maa
he *make-I* come

- as a causative verb **hâi** ให้ is usually placed before the personal pronoun, here **pŏm** ผม *I*
- as a causative verb **hâi** ให้ can be translated into English as *to let, to make, to request, to order* or *to force* depending on the structure of the sentence and how it is said

③ hâi ให้ as a causative compound verb

I will not let you win.

ฉัน ไม่ ยอม ให้ คุณ ชนะ
tʃán mâi *yɔɔm-hâi-khun* tʃáná
I no *allow-let-you* win

- here **hâi** ให้ is used together with another verb **yɔɔm** ยอม *to let* to make the meaning clear
- **yɔɔm-hâi** ยอม ให้ *to let, to allow* is a compound verb

Secret 17 – hâi ให้ in idiomatic expressions

- to use the verb **yɔɔm** ยอม *to let* alone here without **hâi** ให้ is not correct

> **3.1**
> He ordered me to go to work.
> เขา สั่ง ให้ ผม ไป ทำ งาน
> kháu *sàng-hâi* phŏm pai tham-ngaan
> he *order-make* I go do-work

- here **hâi** ให้ is used together with another verb to make the meaning clear

- **sàng-hâi** สั่ง ให้ *to order, to command* is a compound verb

> **4**
> hâi ให้ as a preposition *for*
>
> He bought ice cream for me.
> เขา ซื้อ ไอติม ให้ ฉัน
> kháu súu aitim *hâi* tʃǎn
> he buy ice cream *give* I

- the verb **hâi** ให้ is placed before the personal pronoun, here **tʃǎn** ฉัน *I* at the end of the sentence

- when **hâi** ให้ is placed after the main verb, here **súu** ซื้อ *to buy* and the object, here **aitim** ไอติม *ice cream,* the meaning in English is *for*

- Thai people, however, would understand the verb **hâi** ให้ in this structure as *to give* even though we need to translate it here into English as *for*

D. Simple advice

To translate ideas from one language to another is an art. It is not possible to translate from one language to another on a word for word basis. Every language has idiomatic expressions, and they can't usually be explained in structural terms.

However, in Thai when **hâi** ให้ is used in any statement, it usually expresses a kind of command or urge to get someone to do something.

Using idiomatic expressions is fun. Just learn to use them the right way in the right place!

PART V

More practice with **hâi** ให้

To indicate, to show
แสดง ให้ เห็น
sàdɛɛng-hâi-hĕn

hâi can fix many kinds of problems. hâi says: "When I am between two verbs, which have a similar meaning, everybody will understand the meaning."

ให้ เป็น คน ที่ แก้ ปัญหา ได้ หลาย เรื่อง – ให้ บอก ว่า – เมื่อ ฉัน อยู่ ระหว่าง คำ สอง คำ ที่ มี ความ หมาย คล้ายๆ กัน – ทุก คน เข้า ใจ ความ หมาย แน่ นอน

hâi pen khon thîi kɛ̂ɛ panhăa dâai lăai rûɯang – hâi bɔ̀ɔk-wâa – mûɯa tʃán yùu ráwàang kham sɔ̌ɔng kham thîi mii khwaam-măai khláai-khláai kan – thúk-khon khâu-tsai khwaam-măai nɛ̂ɛ-nɔɔn

hâi be person that fix problem several trouble can – hâi tell that – when I stay between word two word that have subject-meaning similar-similar together – every-person enter-heart matter-subject sure-sleep

SECRET 18

hâi ให้ between two verbs

Usually telling and reporting is expressed in Thai by the pattern **kháu-bɔ̀ɔk wâa...** เขา บอก ว่า *He told me that...* Sometimes **hâi** ให้ is placed between the two verbs in order to make the statement clear and strong.

In this Secret we shall look at a few of the common verbs such as **bɔ̀ɔk-hâi-rúu wâa...** เขา บอก ให้ รู้ ว่า... *to tell that...*

Secret 18 – hâi ให้ between two verbs

A. Sentences

hâi ให้ connecting two verbs

> **I** To show, to indicate – sàdɛɛng-hâi-hĕn แสดง ให้ เห็น
>
> I try to indicate that I do not like this work at all.
>
> ฉัน พยายาม แสดง ให้ เห็น ว่า ไม่ ชอบ งาน นี้ เลย
> tʃán pháyaayaam *sàdɛɛng-hâi-hĕn* wâa mâi tʃɔ́ɔp ngaan níi ləəi
> I try *show-let-see* that no like work this excess

- **sàdɛɛng-hâi-hĕn** แสดง ให้ เห็น *to show, to indicate*
- here **hâi** ให้ is placed between the two verbs **sàdɛɛng** แสดง *to indicate* and **hĕn** เห็น *to see*
- the meaning is clear and strong, *to show, to indicate*

> **Short form**
>
> พยายาม แสดง ว่า ไม่ ชอบ งาน นี้ เลย
> pháyaayaam *sàdɛɛng* wâa mâi tʃɔ́ɔp ngaan níi ləəi
> I try *show* that no like work this excess

- **hâi** ให้ and the other verb **hĕn** เห็น *to see* and the subject **tʃán** ฉัน *I* can be dropped without changing the meaning
- however, **sàdɛɛng wâa** แสดง ว่า is casual and is used when speaking, while **sàdɛɛng-hâi-hĕn wâa** แสดง ให้ เห็น ว่า is more formal

Secret 18 – hâi ให้ between two verbs

2. To tell, to let know – bɔ̀ɔk-hâi-rúu บอก ให้ รู้

He told us that we must leave now.

เขา บอก ให้ รู้ ว่า เรา ต้อง ไป แล้ว
kháu *bɔ̀ɔk-hâi-rúu* wâa rau tɔ̂ng pai lɛ́ɛu
he *tell-let-know* that we must go already

- **bɔ̀ɔk-hâi-rúu** บอก ให้ รู้ *to tell, to let know*
- here **hâi** ให้ *to let* is placed between the two verbs **bɔ̀ɔk** บอก *to tell* and **rúu** รู้ *to know*
- the meaning is clear and strong, *to let know*

Short form

เขา บอก ว่า เรา ต้อง ไป แล้ว
kháu *bɔ̀ɔk-wâa* rau tɔ̂ng pai lɛ́ɛu
he *tell* that we must go already

- **hâi** ให้ and the other verb **rúu** รู้ *to know* can be dropped here without changing the meaning
- **bɔ̀ɔk-wâa** บอก ว่า is usually used casually when speaking instead of **bɔ̀ɔk-hâi-rúu wâa** เขา บอก ให้ รู้ ว่า

3. To inform, to announce – tsɛ̂ɛng-hâi-sâap แจ้ง ให้ ทราบ

He informed us that it's time to go now.

เขา แจ้ง ให้ ทราบ ว่า ได้ เวลา ไป แล้ว
kháu *tsɛ̂ɛng-hâi-sâap* wâa dâai weelaa pai lɛ́ɛu
he *inform-let-know* that get time go already

- **tsɛ̂ɛng-hâi-sâap** แจ้ง ให้ ทราบ *to inform, to announce*
- here **hâi** ให้ is placed between the two verbs **tsɛ̂ɛng** แจ้ง *to inform* and **sâap** ทราบ *to know*

- this kind of statement is often used in formal situations
- the meaning is clear and strong, *to inform, to announce*

Short form

เขา แจ้ง ว่า ได้ เวลา ไป แล้ว
kháu *tsêeng* wâa dâai weelaa pai lέεu
he *inform* that get time go already

- **hâi** ให้ can be dropped without changing the meaning
- however, **tsêeng-wâa** แจ้ง ว่า is casual and is used when speaking while **tsêeng-hâi-sâap-wâa** แจ้ง ให้ ทราบ ว่า is more formal

B. Understanding hâi ให้ between two verbs

- **hâi** ให้ between two verbs
- **hâi** ให้ and verbs with similar meaning

Word order
Put **hâi** ให้ between two verbs as follows:

verb + hâi + verb

sàdεεng-hâi-hěn

indicate-let-see = to show

Usually, the words which go either side of **hâi** ให้ should be a good match with each other. That means that simple ordinary words are not usually mixed with more polite refined words.

This point is not to be taken too seriously, however.

Compare the following three sentences:

Secret 18 – hâi ให้ between two verbs

1
He informed us that we must leave now.
เขา บอก ให้ ทราบ ว่า เรา ต้อง ไป แล้ว
kháu *bɔ̀ɔk-hâi-sâap* wâa rau tɔ̂ng pai lɛ́ɛu
he *tell-let-know* that we must go already

- grammatically this sentence is correct, but the words are not a very good match
- here the verb, **bɔ̀ɔk** บอก *to tell* is an ordinary word, while the verb **sâap** ทราบ *to know* is a more refined word

2
He told us that we must leave now.
เขา บอก ให้ รู้ ว่า เรา ต้อง ไป แล้ว
kháu *bɔ̀ɔk-hâi-rúu* wâa rau tɔ̂ng pai lɛ́ɛu
he *tell-let-know* that we must go already

- here both verbs, **bɔ̀ɔk** บอก *to tell* and **rúu** รู้ *to know*, are ordinary words and are therefore a good match

3
He informed us that we must leave now.
เขา แจ้ง ให้ ทราบ ว่า เรา ต้อง ไป แล้ว
kháu *tsêeng-hâi-sâap* wâa rau tɔ̂ng pai lɛ́ɛu
he *inform-let-know* that we must go already

- here the verbs, **tsêeng** แจ้ง *to inform* and **sâap** ทราบ *to know*, are both refined words and are therefore a good match

Conclusion

hâi ให้ can be placed between two verbs connecting them to form a "distinct" meaning. In this construction the meaning of the three verbs together provides a more sophisticated form of expression. The connected verbs should belong to the same category of verbs. It would not be good style to connect *ordinary every day verbs* with more *refined verbs*.

There doesn't seem to be a similar verb structure in English where three verbs together form one meaning.

On the other hand, in Thai we could use only the main verb alone, and the meaning would be almost the same. Only the colour of the statement is different. See the *short form* sentences above in this section.

C. Language hints

There are quite a few expression where **hâi** ให้ is placed between two verbs. Some expressions are more common and others are used more rarely.

Examples:

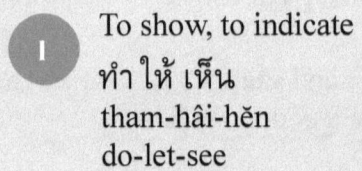

1 To show, to indicate
ทำ ให้ เห็น
tham-hâi-hĕn
do-let-see

- **tham-hâi-hĕn** ทำ ให้ เห็น carries the same meaning as **sàdɛɛng-hâi-hĕn** แสดง ให้ เห็น but is a more casual spoken form

2 To point out
ชี้ ให้ เห็น
tʃǐi-hâi-hěn
point-let-see

- this is a casual spoken form

3 To tell
บอก ให้ ฟัง
bɔ̀ɔk-hâi-fang
tell-tell-hear

- this is a casual spoken form

3.1 To tell (to tell the story/narrative)
เล่า ให้ ฟัง
lâu-hâi-fang
tell-let-hear

- this is often used in writing

4 To explain
อธิบาย ให้ ทราบ
athipaai-hâi-sâap
explain-let-know

- this is polite and formal

5 To inform
เรียน ให้ ทราบ
riian-hâi-sâap
learn-let-know

- this is polite and very formal

D. Simple advice

Thai people would like it if you were able to use at least a few common expressions that were introduced in this Secret. This would show that you have made a serious effort to understand the Thai language and the Thai way.

> One thing to keep in mind is that refined words and expressions are to be used in formal situations only. In day to day situations, common everyday words are preferred when speaking with friends.

It is quite important in Thai that you are able to choose the right word for the relevant situation. If you use words that are not usually used in that particular situation, you may not be immediately understood, no matter how correctly you say them.

Overall, if you manage to be polite, small language mistakes are easily forgiven. It takes some time to adjust yourself to the Thai way.

Let me... May I?
ให้... ได้ไหม
hâi... dâai-mái

If we did not have hâi we would be in trouble. hâi says: "If you want to ask anything, there is no reason to be shy. I can explain everything to you."

ถ้า เรา ไม่ มี ให้ เรา คง จะ แย่ – ให้ บอก ว่า – ถ้า คุณ อยาก ถาม อะไร ไม่ ต้อง อาย ฉัน ตอบ และ อธิบาย ให้ คุณ ได้

thâa rau mâi mii hâi rau khong-tsà yɛ̂ɛ – hâi bɔ̀ɔk-wâa – thâa khun yàak thăam arai mâi tông aai – tʃán tɔ̀ɔp lɛ́ athíbaai hâi khun dâai

if we no have hâi we maybe-will terrible – hâi tell that – if you want ask what no must shy – I reply and explain for you can

SECRET 19

hâi ให้ and questions

hâi ให้ behaves in a question sentence in the same way as it does in the previous example sentences which were not questions.

Questions in Thai are most often formed by putting a question word at the end of a sentence. On some occasions, however, question words are placed at the beginning of a sentence.

A. Sentences

hâi ให้ and simple questions

> **1**
>
> May I -questions – dâai-mái ได้ไหม
>
> Let me think carefully before I let you know, OK?
>
> ให้ ฉัน คิด ให้ รอบ คอบ ก่อน – แล้ว จะ บอก คุณ – ได้ ไหม
>
> *hâi-tʃán-khít hâi-rɔ̂ɔp-khɔ̂ɔp kɔ̀ɔn – lɛ́ɛu tsà bɔ̀ɔk khun – dâai-mái*
>
> *let-I-think let-careful before – then will tell you – can-question*

- **dâai-mái** ได้ไหม question
- here the question is formed by the question words **dâai-mái** ได้ไหม. The **dâai-mái** ได้ไหม *question words* are usually placed at the end of the sentence
- **dâai-mái** ได้ไหม *question words* are polite and make the request softer
- **hâi** ให้ is translated here into English as *to let*

Affirmative reply

> OK, I will let you think first, then tell me.
>
> ฉัน ให้ คุณ คิด ก่อน แล้ว ค่อย บอก ฉัน
>
> tʃán *hâi-khun-khít* kɔ̀ɔn lɛ́ɛu khɔ̂ɔi bɔ̀ɔk tʃán
>
> I *let-you-think* before then gradually tell I

- the reply to this type of question is usually the subject, here **tʃán** ฉัน *I,* + the verb, here **hâi** ให้ *to let*

Short reply

ได้ ค่ะ
dâai khâ
can khâ

- in spoken Thai **dâai khâ** ได้ ค่ะ *yes* would be the most appropriate affirmative reply when the context is understood

Negative reply

ไม่ ได้ ค่ะ
mâi-dâai khâ
no-can khâ

- this statement can be negated by placing **mâi** ไม่ *no* before the verb **dâai** ได้

or

ไม่ ให้ ค่ะ
mâi-hâi khâ
no-let khâ

- this statement can also be negated by placing **mâi** ไม่ *no* before the verb **hâi** ให้

2. Do you -questions – mái ไหม

Can you let me borrow your umbrella?

คุณ ให้ ฉัน ยืม ร่ม ของ คุณ ไหม
khun *hâi-tʃǎn-yuum* rôm khɔ̌ɔng khun *mái*
you *let-I-borrow* umbrella of you *question*

- **mái** ไหม *question word*
- here the question is formed by the question word **mái** ไหม

- **mái** ไหม *question word* is usually placed at the end of the sentence
- **mái** ไหม *question word* is more direct and perhaps not so polite as the **dâai-mái** ได้ไหม *question word*
- **hâi** ให้ is translated here into English as *to let*

> **Affirmative reply**
>
> Yes, you can borrow it.
>
> ฉัน ให้ คุณ ยืม
> tʃǎn *hâi-khun-yɯɯm*
> I *let-you-borrow*

- the reply to this type of question is usually the subject, here **tʃǎn** ฉัน *I,* + the verb, here **hâi** ให้ *to let*

> **Short reply**
>
> ฉัน ให้
> tʃǎn *hâi*
> I *let*

- usually in reply the sentence is cut short when the context is clear

> **Negative reply**
>
> ไม่ ให้ ค่ะ
> *mâi-hâi* khâ
> *no-let* khâ

- this statement can be negated by placing **mâi** ไม่ *no* before the verb **hâi** ให้

Secret 19 – hâi ให้ and questions

> **3** Or not -questions – rú-plàau รึ เปล่า
> Will he let you go out on a trip or not?
> เขา ให้ คุณ ไป เที่ยว รึ เปล่า
> kháu *hâi-khun-pai* thîiau *rú-plàau*
> he *let-you-go* travel *or not*

- **rú-plàau** รึ เปล่า *or not* -question
- here the question is formed by the question words **rú-plàau** รึ เปล่า *or not*
- question words **rú-plàau** รึ เปล่า are usually placed at the end of the sentence
- question words **rú-plàau** รึ เปล่า are more demanding than question words **dâai-mái** ได้ไหม or **mái** ไหม
- it indicates that a *yes* or *no* reply should be given
- **hâi** ให้ is translated here into English as *to let*

Affirmative reply

> Yes, he let me go on a trip.
> เขา ให้ ฉัน ไป เที่ยว
> kháu *hâi-tʃǎn-pai* thîiau
> he *let-I-go* trip

- the reply to this type of question is usually the subject, here **kháu** เขา *he*, + the verb, here **hâi** ให้ *to let*

Short reply

> เขา ให้
> kháu *hâi*
> he *let*

- usually in reply the sentence is cut short when the context is clear

Negative reply

ไม่ ให้ ค่ะ
mâi-hâi khâ
no-let khâ

- this statement can be negated by placing **mâi** ไม่ *no* before the verb **hâi** ให้

or simply

เปล่า
plàau
not

- often to questions made with **rú-plàau** รึ เปล่า the negative reply is simply **plàau** เปล่า *no*

4 Who-questions – khrai ใคร

Who gave this book to you?
ใคร ให้ หนังสือ เล่ม นี้ กับ คุณ
khrai-hâi-năngsŭu lêm níi kàp khun
who-give-book piece this with you

- **khrai hâi** ใคร ให้ *Who gave?*
- here the question is formed by a question word **khrai** ใคร *who*. **khrai** ใคร *who* is usually placed at the beginning of the sentence
- **hâi** ให้ is translated here into English as *to give*

Secret 19 – hâi ให้ and questions

Affirmative reply

> My friend gave it to me.
> เพื่อน ของ ฉัน ให้
> phûuan khɔ̆ɔng tʃán *hâi*
> friend of I *give*

- the reply to this type of question is usually the subject, here **phûuan** เพื่อน *friend* + the verb, here **hâi** ให้ *to give*

Short reply

> เพื่อน ให้
> phûuan *hâi*
> friend *give*

- note that usually in reply the sentence is cut short when the context is clear

Negative reply

> ไม่ มี ใคร ให้ ค่ะ
> mâi mii khrai *hâi* khâ
> no have who *give* khâ

- this statement can be negated by placing **mâi** ไม่ *no* before the verb **mii** มี

B. Understanding hâi ให้ and questions

- **hâi** ให้ and questions
- **hâi** ให้ behaves in a question sentence the same way as it does in previous example sentences which were not questions

Word order

It is important to ensure that we use question words correctly. Quite often question words in Thai are placed at the end of the sentence.

> subject + hâi ให้... + dâai-mái   ได้ไหม   *questions*
> subject + hâi ให้... + mái   ไหม   *questions*
> subject + hâi ให้... + rú-plàau   รึเปล่า   *questions*

There are, however, some question words which are placed at the beginning of a sentence.

Example:

> khrai + hâi... ใครให้... *who gave...?*

Some question words can be placed either at the beginning or at the end of a sentence. See more about this in the language hints in the section below.

> **Conclusion**
>
> When you know how to use **hâi** ให้ in a non question sentence or statement, then it is not difficult to use **hâi** ให้ in a question.
>
> Here the important point is to use question words correctly. When **hâi** ให้ is used in a question, the answer usually also contains the verb **hâi** ให้.

C. Language hints

There are many more ways to form a question in Thai. It may be useful for you to know the following:

 Question words at the end of a sentence

Secret 19 – hâi ให้ and questions

Questions in Thai are usually formed in such a way that the question word comes at the end of the sentence. Here we have a few examples:

mái	ไหม	*question word*
tʃâi-mái	ใช่ ไหม	*right?*
rǔu-plàau	หรือ เปล่า	*or not*
arai	อะไร	*what*
arai-ná	อะไร นะ	*what, what did you say, sorry*
thâu-rài	เท่า ไหร่	*how much*
thîi-nǎi	ที่ ไหน	*where*
yang-ngai	ยัง ไง	*how*
lɛ́ɛu-rǔu-yang	แล้ว หรือ ยัง	*already* or *not*
lâ	ล่ะ	
ná	นะ	

b) Question words at the *beginning* or at the *end* of the sentence.

Some question words can be placed either at the beginning or the end of a sentence. The most common are:

khrai	ใคร	*who*
mûua-rài	เมื่อ ไหร่	*when*

Examples:

khrai	ใคร	*who*

> **1** Who told you?
> ใคร บอก
> *khrai* bɔ̀ɔk
> *who* tell

- **khrai** ใคร *who*

- **khrai** ใคร *who* is usually placed at the beginning of the sentence

But

Secret 19 – hâi ให้ and questions

> **1.1** Who are you?
> คุณ เป็น ใคร
> khun pen *khrai*
> you be *who*

- **khrai** ใคร *who*
- in sentences like this **khrai** ใคร *who* is placed at the end

mûua-rài เมื่อไหร่ *when*

mûua-rài เมื่อไหร่ *when* is usually placed at the end of a sentence, but for empathetic statements the question word **mûua-rài** เมื่อไหร่ can also be placed at the beginning of the sentence

Examples:

> **2** When are you going to Phuket?
> คุณ จะ ไป ภูเก็ต เมื่อไหร่
> khun tsà pai phuukèt *mûua-rài*
> you will go Phuket *when*

- **mûua-rài** เมื่อไหร่ *when*
- here the question **mûua-rài** เมื่อไหร่ is placed at the end of the sentence
- going to Phuket is emphasised

> **2.1** When are you going to Phuket?
> เมื่อไหร่ คุณ จะ ไป ภูเก็ต
> *mûua-rài* khun tsà pai phuukèt
> *when* you will go Phuket

- **mûua-rài** เมื่อไหร่ *when*

Secret 19 – hâi ให้ and questions

- here the question word **mûua-rài** เมื่อไหร่ is emphasised and is therefore placed at the beginning of the sentence

c) Question word which follows *some special rules*.

Thai people apply these rules intuitively. Please take a note of the following. In some special cases **thammai** ทำไม *why* is placed at the beginning of the sentence.

Examples:

> **1**
> Why do you have to go?
> ทำไม คุณ ต้อง ไป
> *thammai* khun tông pai
> *why* you must go

- **thammai** ทำไม *why*

> **1.1**
> Why are you going?
> ทำไม คุณ ถึง ไป
> *thammai* khun thǔng pai
> *why* you reach go

- **thammai** ทำไม *why*

> **1.2**
> Why do you want to go?
> ทำไม คุณ อยาก ไป
> *thammai* khun yàak pai
> *why* you want go

- **thammai** ทำไม *why*
- when there is a modal verb such as **tông** ต้อง, **thǔng** ถึง and **yàak** อยาก in the sentence, the question word **thammai** ทำไม is placed at the beginning of the sentence

> **1.3** Why aren't you going?
> ทำไม คุณ ไม่ ไป
> *thammai* khun mâi pai
> *why* you no go

- **thammai** ทำไม *why*
- in negative sentences **thammai** ทำไม is usually placed at the beginning of the sentence

> **1.4** Why aren't you going?
> คุณ จะ ไม่ ไป ทำไม
> khun tsà mâi pai *thammai*
> you will no go *why*

- **thammai** ทำไม *why*
- in negative sentences **thammai** ทำไม may also be placed at the end of the sentence
- to put **thammai** ทำไม in the negative statement at the end of the sentence is grammatically correct, but not very common in speaking

> **1.5** Why are you going?
> คุณ จะ ไป ทำไม
> khun tsà pai *thammai*
> you will go *why*

- **thammai** ทำไม *why*
- in affirmative sentences **thammai** ทำไม *why* is usually placed at the end of the sentence

D. Simple advice

There is one more useful question word to be learned:

- **kìi** กี่ *how many*

This question word is used somewhat differently from those reviewed in the above language hints section.

Examples:

> **1** How many students came?
> นัก เรียน มา กี่ คน
> nák riian maa *kìi-khon*
> student come *how-many person*

- **kìi** กี่ *how many*
- **kìi** กี่ is a special case and is usually placed after the main verb and before the classifier
- **kìi** กี่ is placed in this example before the classifier, **khon** คน *people*

> **2** **Short form**
> มา กี่ คน
> maa *kìi-khon*
> come *how-many person*

- **kìi** กี่ *how many*
- the main word **nák-riian** นัก เรียน *student* may be omitted, and only the classifier is used if the meaning is understood from the context

Secret 20 – hâi ให้ and negatives statements

Won't let
ไม่ ให้
mâi-hâi

hâi is a person, who can agree easily, but she says: "Really, I cannot allow bad people to hurt me."

ให้ เป็น คน ที่ ยอม คน อื่น ได้ ง่ายๆ แต่ ว่า – เขา บอก ว่า – บาง ครั้ง ฉัน ก็ ไม่ อยาก ให้ คน ที่ ไม่ ดี ทำให้ ฉัน เจ็บ

hâi pen khon thîi yɔɔm khon ʉ̀ʉn dâai ngâai-ngâai tɛ̀ɛ-wâa – kháu bɔ̀ɔk-wâa – baang-khráng tʃán gɔ̂ɔ mâi-yàak-hâi khon thîi mâi dii tham-hâi tʃán tsèp

hâi be person that allow person other can easy-easy but-that – she tell that – some-time I also no-want-let person that no good do-make I hurt

Secret 20

hâi ให้ and negative statements

In Thai affirmative statements are generally negated by putting the word **mâi** ไม่ *no* in front of **hâi** ให้ or any other main verb.

Secret 20 – hâi ให้ and negatives statements

A. Sentences

Making negative statements

1 Don't want – mâi-yàak-hâi... ไม่ อยาก ให้

I don't want anybody to see.
ฉัน ไม่ อยาก ให้ ใคร เห็น
tʃǎn *mâi-yàak-hâi-khrai* hěn
I *no-want-let-who* see

- **mâi-yàak-hâi** ไม่ อยาก ให้ *don't want*
- here the negative meaning is expressed by **mâi-yàak-hâi** ไม่ อยาก ให้ *don't want*
- it is placed before the object, here **khrai** ใคร *who, anybody*
- note that **yàak** อยาก *to want* must always be followed by the verb, here **hâi** ให้

Short form

ไม่ อยาก ให้ ใคร เห็น
mâi-yàak-hâi-khrai hěn
no-want-let-who see

- **mâi-yàak-hâi** ไม่ อยาก ให้ *don't want*
- the subject, **tʃǎn** ฉัน *I,* can be omitted if understood from the context

2 Don't let, won't let – mâi-hâi ไม่ ให้

He won't let me go on a trip.
เขา ไม่ ให้ ฉัน ไป เที่ยว
kháu *mâi-hâi-tʃǎn* pai thîiau
he *no-let-I* go trip

Secret 20 – hâi ให้ and negatives statements

- **mâi-hâi** ไม่ ให้ *won't let*
- in this statement the negative meaning is expressed by **mâi-hâi** ไม่ ให้ *won't let*
- it is placed before the object, here **tʃán** ฉัน *I*
- the word **mâi** ไม่ *no* is placed in front of **hâi** ให้

> **Short form**
>
> เขา ไม่ ให้ ไป เที่ยว
> kháu *mâi-hâi* pai thîiau
> he *no-let* go trip

- **mâi-hâi** ไม่ ให้ *won't let*
- the object, **tʃán** ฉัน *I*, can be omitted when understood from the context

> **3** Cannot – mâi-dâai ไม่ ได้
>
> Tell him that he cannot go to the bar.
> บอก ให้ เขา รู้ ว่า ไป บาร์ เบียร์ ไม่ ได้
> *bɔ̀ɔk-hâi-kháu* rúu wâa pai baa biia *mâi-dâai*
> tell-make-he know that go bar beer *no-can*

- **mâi-dâai** ไม่ ได้ *cannot*
- in this sentence the negative meaning is expressed by **mâi-dâai** ไม่ ได้ *cannot*
- **mâi-dâai** ไม่ ได้ *cannot* is usually placed at the end of a sentence meaning *not allowed* or *not having a permission to*

> **Short form**
>
> บอก เขา ว่า ไป บาร์ เบียร์ ไม่ ได้
> *bɔ̀ɔk-kháu* wâa pai baa biia *mâi-dâai*
> tell he that go bar beer *no-can*

- **mâi-dâai** ไม่ ได้ *cannot*
- the verbs **hâi** ให้ and **rúu** รู้ *to know* can be omitted without changing the meaning
- only the colour of the sentence is slightly changed

B. Understanding hâi ให้ and negative statements

- **hâi** ให้ and negatives
- **mâi-hâi** *no-let, do not*

Word order

The positive phrase can be negated by putting the word **mâi** ไม่ in front of **hâi** ให้ or **mâi-dâai** ไม่ ได้ at the end of the sentence as follows:

1
Subject + *mâi-hâi-tʃăn...*

He + *no-let-I* = He does not let me...

He does not let me go on a trip.

เขา ไม่ ให้ ฉัน ไป เที่ยว
kháu *mâi-hâi-tʃăn* pai thîiau
he *no-let-I* go trip

- using **mâi-hâi** ไม่ ให้ + object is direct and strong negative statement

2
Subject + *mâi-yàak-hâi* + object

I + *no-want-let* + anybody = I don't want anybody...

I don't want anybody to see.

ฉัน ไม่ อยาก ให้ ใคร เห็น
tʃăn *mâi-yàak-hâi-khrai* hĕn
I *no-want-let-who* see

- **mâi-yàak-hâi** ไม่ อยาก ให้ *don't want*

Secret 20 – hâi ให้ and negatives statements

- when there is a modal verb like **yàak** อยาก *to want*, then **mâi** ไม่ *no* is placed in front of it

> **3**
>
> *bɔ̀ɔk-hâi-kháu* + verb... + *mâi-dâai*
>
> *Tell-make-he* + know... + *mâi-dâai* = Tell him! He cannot go.
>
> Tell him that that he can't go.
>
> บอก ให้ เขา รู้ ว่า ไป ไม่ ได้
> *bɔ̀ɔk-hâi-kháu* rúu wâa pai *mâi-dâai*
> *tell-make-he* know that go *no-can*

- here the affirmative sentence is negated at the end of the sentence by **mâi-dâai** ไม่ ได้

> **4**
>
> *yàa-hâi* + object + verb
>
> *Don't-let* + child + play = Do not let children play...
>
> Don't let children play in the evening.
>
> อย่า ให้ ลูก เล่น ตอน ค่ำ
> *yàa-hâi* lûuk lên tɔɔn-khâm
> *no-let* child play at evening

- **yàa-hâi** อย่า ให้ *don't*

- sometimes other verbs like **yàa-hâi** อย่า ให้ *don't*, which usually denotes the direct command *don't,* is used to indicate that the action should not take place

- using **yaa** อย่า + verb is very strong and direct. It is also a command

Conclusion

hâi ให้ can be negated by placing the word **mâi** ไม่ *no* in front of it.

In direct commands the word **yàa** อย่า *don't* can be used instead of **mâi** ไม่ *no*. Note, however, that using **yaa** อย่า + **hâi** ให้ is quite strong denial.

Using polite ending particles in negative sentences whenever possible is quite important in Thai.

There are occasions when it is more natural to use the phrase **mâi-dâai** ไม่ได้ *can't* at the end of the sentence to form a negative meaning.

C. Language hints

a) The following words are usually used to indicate that the action should not take place.

Words used to negate affirmative phrases.

1 mâi ไม่ *no*

- **mâi** ไม่ *no* is a general way to convert the positive phrase into a negative statement. It is usually placed before the main verb

2 plàau เปล่า *no*

- **plàau** เปล่า *no* is commonly used in replies to **rŭu-plàau** หรือเปล่า *or not* -questions

3 mâi-tʃâi ไม่ใช่ *no*

- **mâi-tʃâi** ไม่ ใช่ *no* is commonly used in replies

> **4** mâi-dâai ไม่ ได้ *cannot*

- **mâi-dâai** ไม่ ได้ is another construction, which can be translated into English as *not able to, can't, should not, not possible*. It usually comes at the end of the sentence

> **5** mâi-hâi ไม่ ให้ *do not give, do not let*

- when **mâi** ไม่ *no* is placed before the verb **hâi** ให้, the meaning becomes *don't give* or *don't let*

> **6** mâi-au ไม่ เอา *do not want*

- when **mâi** ไม่ *no* is placed before the verb **au** เอา, the meaning becomes *don't want*

> **7** yàa อย่า usually indicates a direct command, such as *do not...*

- **yàa** อย่า is usually placed in front of the main verb

b) Special cases

> **1** He is not a good person.
> เขา ไม่ ดี
> kháu *mâi-dii*
> he *no-good*

- **mâi** ไม่ can be placed before an adjective since adjectives in Thai also play the role of a verb

Secret 20 – hâi ให้ and negatives statements

> **2**
> He is not a good person.
> เขา ไม่ ใช่ คน ดี
> kháu *mâi-tʃâi* khon dii
> he *no-yes* person good

- when there is a classifier then **mâi-tʃâi** ไม่ใช่ is usually placed before the object, here **khon** คน *person*

> **3**
> He did not go on a trip.
> เขา ไม่ ได้ ไป เที่ยว
> kháu *mâi-dâai* pai thîiau
> he *no-get* go trip

- **mâi-dâai** ไม่ ได้ = past tense
- **mâi-dâai** ไม่ ได้ is often used in a negative sentence to point out that the action in the past did not take place
- it can also mean *did not have a chance*
- when expressing a past tense with **mâi-dâai** ไม่ได้, it is placed before the main verb, here **pai** ไป to go

D. Simple advice

Negative statements in Thai are used somewhat differently from their usage in European languages. Perhaps the difference comes from the fact that languages often reflect the cultural behaviour of the people in the country.

Generally, it can be said that one should not use negative statements, involving negative feelings, directly face to face in Thailand. When negative statements are used, they are used in positive and sometimes roundabout ways. One should not step on anybody's toes, and everybody should be respected. In other words "saving face" is an important factor when interacting with Thai people.

Usually negative phrases involving negative feelings are not spoken directly to another person "you". They are often used to refer to a first person "I" or third person "he or she".

Examples:

> **1** Don't do like that!
> อย่า ทำ แบบ นี้
> *yàa-tham* bèɛp-níi
> *no-do* like-this!

- this a direct negative statement
- this would be considered harsh and somewhat rude in Thai when said face to face

> **2** I think that like this is better.
> ผม คิด ว่า แบบ นี้ ดี กว่า
> phŏm khít wâa bèɛp-níi *dii-gwàa*
> I think that like this *good-more*

- this is a roundabout Thai way to express the same

> **3** Please don't forget!
> อย่า ลืม นะ
> yàa-luum *ná*
> no-forget *ná!*

- using **ná** นะ!
- negative statements are usually softened by polite end particles. This way negative statements can be used in a more positive way

4 He told me not to go to the bar.
เขา บอก ว่า ไม่ ให้ ฉัน / ผม ไป บาร์ เบียร์
kháu bɔ̀ɔk-wâa mâi-hâi tʃán pai baa biia
he tell-that no-let I go bar beer

- if the negative statement is related to a third person it is more acceptable since it is an indirect way of expressing feelings

5 I am not good at all.
ผม ไม่ เก่ง เลย
phǒm *mâi gèng* ləəi
I *no good* excess

- downgrading oneself

- actually, here the negative statement is used as a polite way *to downgrade* oneself. As you may have already learned it is not polite in Thai culture to boost your own ego. To be humble is considered to have good manners. In the West things can be somewhat different

- foreigners are perhaps already seen as people who may have some skills and a bit of money. Thai people will respect you much more if you can "downgrade" the fact and be simple and ordinary

- for example, Thai people will never get tired telling you how well you speak the Thai language. The appropriate way to respond to that would be to say **mâi kèng rɔ̀ɔk** ไม่ เก่ง หรอก *Not good at all*

Secret 21 – hâi ให้ several times in one statement

For you... for me...
ให้ คุณ... ให้ ฉัน
hâi khun...hâi tʃăn...

---

hâi is a person who likes to show off. hâi says: "Everybody should have a chance to shine and be oneself."

ให้ เป็น คน ที่ ชอบ แสดง ออก – ให้ บอก ว่า – ทุก คน ควร จะ มี โอกาส ฉาย แวว และ แสดง ความ เป็น ตัว เอง ออก มา

hâi pen khon thîi tʃɔ̂ɔp sàdɛɛng-ɔ̀ɔk – hâi bɔ̀ɔk-wâa – thúk-khon khuuan-tsà mii oogàat tʃăai-wɛɛu lé sàdɛɛng khwaam-pen tuua-eeng ɔ̀ɔk-maa

hâi be person that like show-out – hâi tell that – every-person should-will have chance shine-bright and matter-be body-self out-come

Secret 21

hâi ให้ can play different roles in a single statement

hâi ให้ is often used in short sentences and structures, but it also appears in longer sentences. Sometimes it can even appear two or three times, with different meanings, in a single statement.

Secret 21 – hâi ให้ several times in one statement

A. Sentences

hâi ให้ can have different roles in one single statement

Examples:

> **1** You...for me – hâi khun...hâi tʃǎn ให้ คุณ...ให้ ฉัน
>
> There is one thing I would like you to buy for me, a beautiful dress.
>
> ของ อย่าง หนึ่ง ที่ ฉัน อยาก จะ ให้ คุณ ซื้อ ให้ ฉัน คือ เสื้อ ผ้า สวยๆ
> khɔ̌ɔng yàang-nùng thîi tʃǎn *yàak-tsà-hâi-khun* súu *hâi-tʃǎn* khuu sûua-phâa sǔuai-sǔuai
> thing sort-one that I *want-will-make-you* buy *give-I* be shirt-cloth beautiful-beautiful

- **hâi khun...hâi tʃǎn** ให้ คุณ...ให้ ฉัน *you...for me*
- here **hâi** ให้ is first used in the verb compound **yàak-tsà-hâi** อยาก จะ ให้ *would like to*
- it is placed before the pronoun **khun** คุณ *you*
- the second **hâi** ให้ is used as a preposition *for* **hâi tʃǎn** ให้ ฉัน *for me*

> **Short form**
>
> อยาก จะ ให้ คุณ ซื้อ เสื้อ ผ้า สวยๆ ให้
> *yàak-tsà-hâi-khun* súu sûua-phâa sǔuai-sǔuai *hâi*
> *want-will-make-you* buy shirt-cloth beautiful-beautiful *give*

- the short form is often more simple and direct
- the first part of the sentence, **khɔ̌ɔng yàang-nùng thîi** ของ อย่าง หนึ่ง ที่ *there is one thing*, can be left out when it is understood from the context

- similarly, the subject **tʃán** ฉัน *I*, the object **tʃán** ฉัน *for me* and the verb **khuu** คือ *is,* can be left out when speaking if understood from the context

> **2** To inform us – tsêeng-hâi-sâap แจ้ง ให้ ทราบ
>
> He informed us that he wants everybody to learn to swim.
>
> เขา แจ้ง ให้ ทราบ ว่า เขา ต้องการ ให้ ทุก คน ว่าย น้ำ เป็น
>
> kháu *tsêeng-hâi-sâap* wâa kháu *tôngkaan-hâi-thúk-khon* wâai-náam pen
>
> he *inform-let-know* that he *must-make-every-person* swim-water be

- **tsêeng-hâi-sâap...hâi thúk-khon** แจ้ง ให้ ทราบ...ให้ ทุก คน to *inform...everybody*
- here we have **hâi** ให้ first between the two verbs **tsêeng** แจ้ง *to inform* and **sâap** ทราบ *to know*
- the second **hâi** ให้ is used as a compound verb together with the verb **tông-kaan** ต้องการ *to want*
- **tông-kaan-hâi** ต้องการ ให้ is placed before the pronoun **thúk-khon** ทุก คน *everybody*

> **Short form**
>
> เขา บอก ว่า เขา ต้องการ ให้ ทุก คน ว่ายน้ำ เป็น
>
> kháu bɔ̀ɔk-wâa kháu *tông-kaan-hâi-thúk-khon* wâai-náam pen
>
> He *tell-that* he want *must-make-every-person* swim-water be

- **bɔ̀ɔk-wâa** บอก ว่า *to tell that* is a casual spoken form compared to **tsêeng-hâi-sâap- wâa** แจ้ง ให้ ทราบ ว่า *to inform that,* which is quite formal

> **3** I give you this...to finish...well –
> hâi khun...hâi-sèt...hâi-dii ให้ คุณ...ให้ เสร็จ...ให้ ดี
>
> I give you this machine so that you can finish your job both quickly and well.
>
> ฉัน ให้ เครื่อง มือ นี้ กับ คุณ เพื่อ จะ ทำ ให้ งาน คุณ เสร็จ เร็วๆ และ ให้ ดี ด้วย
> tʃán *hâi* khrûuang muu-nii kàp khun phûua-tsà *tham-hâi* ngaan khun sèt reu-reu lé *hâi-dii* dûuai
> I *give* machine-this with you in order-will *do-make* work you finish fast-fast and *make-good* also

- **hâi khun...tham-hâi...hâi-dii** ให้ คุณ...ทำ ให้...ให้ ดี *to you...to make...well*

- here **hâi** ให้ *to give* is used first as a main verb *to give*

- the second **hâi** ให้ as a compound verb together with the verb **tham** ทำ *to do* is placed before the noun **ngaan** งาน *job, work*

- **tham-hâi** ทำ ให้ in English means *to make*

- the third **hâi** ให้ is placed before the adjective **dii** ดี *good* changing it to an adverb, *well*

> **Short form**
>
> ฉัน ให้ – ทำ ให้ เสร็จ เร็วๆ และ ให้ ดี ด้วย
> tʃán *hâi* – *tham-hâi* sèt reu-reu lé *hâi-dii* dûuai
> I *give* – *do-make* finish fast-fast and *make-good* also

- the first object **khrûuang-níi** เครื่อง นี้ *this machine* can be left out if understood from the context

- also the words **khun** คุณ *you* and **ngaan-níi** งาน นี้ *this job* can be left out if they are understood from the context

- this is a more intuitive and shorter way to express the same thing as in the main sentence above

B. Understanding hâi ให้ in different roles in one sentence

- **hâi** ให้ can appear several times in one sentence or statement with different meanings

Word order

> Subject + *yàak-hâi-khun* + verb + *hâi-tʃǎn*
>
> I + *want-make-you* + buy + *give-I* = I want you to buy for me...

By using this book to learn how to use **hâi** ให้, you will also learn many more words, which are used with **hâi** ให้, and also some grammar and general language points, which will be helpful in advancing your Thai studies.

Sometimes the semantic boundaries of **hâi** ให้ are not directly comparable with English. Yet, a translation of a sentence with **hâi** ให้ is always possible if the context is understood clearly. There may be cases when the translation of the word **hâi** ให้ into English (as distinct from a sentence containing it) could be redundant.

Conclusion

It is an art to use the verb **hâi** ให้, particularly when it is used for different English meanings in one single sentence or statement.

When we try to penetrate into the psychology of **hâi** ให้ with the English language, and if we had to choose only three words to describe the meaning of hâi ให้, they would be *to give, to let* and *to make*.

However, then we would need to expand the semantic boundaries of these three English words *to give, to let* and *to make* far beyond of their normal usage.

Often it would make sense to translate hâi ให้ into English as *to give, to let* or *to make,* but some other times we need to use English words such as *for* and *until* in order to get the correct meaning.

Also when hâi ให้ is used as a compound verb together with other verbs, the meaning is coloured by the other verb.

C. Language hints

a) Apart from idiomatic expressions and special cases, we may summarise the usage of **hâi** ให้ in the sentence as follows:

Examples:

> **1**
> He gave potatoes to me.
> เขา ให้ มัน ฝรั่ง กับ ฉัน
> kháu *hâi-man-fàràng* gàp tʃǎn
> he *gave-potato* with I

- **hâi** ให้ as *to give*
- in this structure **hâi** ให้ points towards things

Secret 21 – hâi ให้ several times in one statement

- here the action is *to give,* and **hâi** ให้ is placed before direct object, **man** มัน *it*
- to whom the object is given comes after

> **2**
> He bought it for me.
> เขา ซื้อ ให้
> kháu súu *hâi*
> he buy *for*

- **hâi** ให้ as *for*
- in this structure **hâi** ให้ points towards persons
- here the action is *to buy for,* and **hâi** ให้ is placed before the direct object, *me, you* or *Peter etc...* which are here understood from the context and therefore dropped
- depending on the context, this sentence could also be translated into English as:

  He bought it and gave it to me.
  He bought it for you.
  He bought it for Peter
  etc.

> **3**
> I let you go!
> ฉัน ให้ คุณ ไป
> tʃán *hâi-khun* pai
> I *let-you* go

- **hâi** ให้ as *to let*
- in this structure **hâi** ให้ points towards persons
- here the action is *to let,* and **hâi** ให้ is placed before the pronoun, **khun** คุณ *you*
- depending on the context, this sentence could also be translated into English as:

Secret 21 – hâi ให้ several times in one statement

I request you to go.
I'll make you go!

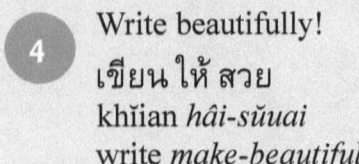

4 Write beautifully!
เขียน ให้ สวย
khĭian *hâi-sŭuai*
write *make-beautiful*

- **hâi** ให้ before adjectives = adverb
- in this structure **hâi** ให้ points towards how the action should be carried out
- here the action is a command *Write beautifully!*
- **hâi** ให้ is placed before an adjective, **sŭuai** สวย *beautiful*

b) It would be good to know the difference between **khɯɯ** คือ and **pen** เป็น *to be*

They are used in a similar way but there are some essential differences in usage.

Both these words are commonly used to link two nouns or a pronoun and a noun in the sentence and can be translated in English as "to be" as follows:

Pronoun + pen เป็น or khɯɯ คือ + noun

(He)   (is)   (doctor)

Both **khɯɯ** คือ and **pen** เป็น always need to be followed by a noun while **pen** เป็น in some special idioms like "**pen sòot** เป็นโสด *to be single*" can also be followed by an adjective.

pen เป็น is usually used to make a definite statement while **khɯɯ** คือ is used more with hesitation, explanation and clarification while explaining something. It often leaves something open or "up in the air".

khuu wâa คือ ว่า is translated into English as *namely, for instance, for example, it is like that...*

Examples:

> **1** He is a doctor.
> เขา เป็น หมอ
> kháu *pen* mɔ̌ɔ
> he *be* doctor

or

> **2** He is a doctor.
> เขา คือ หมอ
> kháu *khuu* mɔ̌ɔ
> he *be* doctor

- in the above examples the verb **khuu** คือ meaning *to be* is used in a similar way as **pen** เป็น

- the translation into English is exactly the same. However, the meaning is not exactly the same in Thai. **khâu khuu mɔ̌ɔ** เขา คือ หมอ can be more respectful

- it is not only a simple direct statement as is the case with **khâu pen mɔ̌ɔ** เขา เป็น หมอ

- however, the usage of **pen** เป็น *to be* is much wider. It can be used in a variety of ways in the sentence as follows:

> **3** Note that pen เป็น cannot usually be followed by an adjective. You cannot say: **Warning**
>
> kháu pen dii
> เขา เป็น ดี
> he is good

Add a noun and the statement is fine:

> kháu pen khon dii
> เขา เป็น คน ดี
> he is a good person

Or drop the word pen เป็น and say:

> kháu dii
> เขา ดี
> he is a good person

- that is the short form for the same

4 pen เป็น is commonly used when referring to diseases and body conditions as follows:

pen khâi เป็น ไข้ *to have a fever*
pen wàt เป็น หวัด *to have a cold*
pen máreng เป็น มะเร็ง *to have a cancer*
pen rôok เป็น โรค *to have a disease*

5 In some special cases pen เป็น can be followed by an adjective such as

pen sòot เป็น โสด *to be single*

6 Note that pen เป็น *to be* can also be translated after a verb as *having knowledge how to do* something. It comes usually at the end of the sentence.

rau wâai-náam pen เรา ว่าย น้ำ เป็น
we can swim or *we have a skill to swim*

D. Simple advice

One simple rule to keep in mind is that when **hâi** ให้ is used as a main verb, it means *to give*.

Secondly, when **hâi** ให้ is used in a sentence as a helping verb before the main verb and is placed before the pronoun, it is usually then used as a causative verb meaning *to let, to make, to request, to order, etc.*

Thirdly, when **hâi** ให้ stands in a sentence after the main verb, it is often translated into English as a preposition meaning *for* or *to*. Then it is usually placed before the personal pronoun at the end of the sentence. Here Thai people would think in terms of *to give*. The English translation would be *I bought it for you*. Thai would say I bought it *to give* you.

Fourthly, when **hâi** ให้ is used as a compound verb together with other verbs, the meaning is also coloured by the other verb.

Could *you help me*?
ขอ คุณ ให้ ช่วย
khɔ̌ɔ khun hâi tʃûuai

hâi is a rather smart person. hâi says: "Try to understand that two sentences can have the same meaning even though they are not written the same way."

ให้ เป็น คน ที่ ค่อน ข้าง ฉลาด – ให้ บอก ว่า – พยายาม เข้า ใจ ว่า สอง ประโยค นี้ มี ความ หมาย เหมือน กัน แม้ ว่า จะ เขียน ไม่ เหมือน กัน

hâi pen khon thîi khɔ̂n-khâang tʃàlàat – hâi bɔ̀ɔk-wâa – pháyaayaam khâu-tsai wâa – sɔ̌ɔng pràyòok níi mii khwaam-mǎai mǔɐan-kan mɛ́ɛ-wâa tsà khǐian mâi mǔɐan-kan

hâi be person that toward-side smart – hâi tell that – try enter-heart that two sentence this have matter-aim same-together even-that will write no same-together

SECRET 22

hâi ให้ as a compound verb and *changing the word order*

The position for **hâi** ให้ can be changed in a sentence with some verbs such as **khɔ̌ɔ** ขอ *to ask*, **bɔ̀ɔk** บอก *to tell*, **tuuan** เตือน *to warn*, when **hâi** ให้ is placed after the object instead of before the object.

It depends on the situation and the speaker which structure is used. Changing the word order does not change the meaning of the sentence whether you use:

khɔ̌ɔ-khun-hâi   ขอ คุณ ให้   *I ask you to*
khɔ̌ɔ-hâi-khun   ขอ ให้ คุณ   *I ask you to*

hâi ให้ and changing the word order in compounds

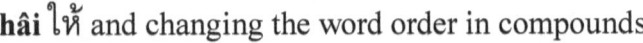

> **I** Asking you to... – khɔ̌ɔ-khun-hâi... ขอ คุณ ให้
>
> Could you help me a little?
>
> ฉัน ขอ คุณ ให้ ช่วย หน่อย ได้ไหม
> tʃán *khɔ̌ɔ-khun-hâi-tʃûuai* nɔ̀i dâai-mái
> I *ask-you-make-help* little can-question

- **khɔ̌ɔ-khun-hâi** ขอ คุณ ให้ *to ask you to*
- here the object, **khun** คุณ *you,* is placed between the verb **khɔ̌ɔ** ขอ *to ask* and **hâi** ให้

> **1.1** A different word order
>
> Could you help me a little?
>
> ฉัน ขอ ให้ คุณ ช่วย หน่อย ได้ไหม
> tʃán *khɔ̌ɔ-hâi-khun* tʃûuai nɔ̀i dâai-mái
> I *ask-make-you* help little can-question

- **khɔ̌ɔ-hâi-khun** ฉัน ขอ ให้ คุณ *to ask you to*
- **hâi** ให้ can also be placed before the object, **khun** คุณ *you* and directly after the verb **khɔ̌ɔ** ขอ *to ask*
- the meaning in this sentence is the same as in the above sentences **khɔ̌ɔ-khun-hâi** ขอ คุณ ให้ *to ask you to*
- it depends on the speaker and perhaps also on the context which structure is used

Secret 22 – hâi ให้ and changing the word order

2. Tell him to... – bɔ̀ɔk-kháu-hâi... บอก เขา ให้

Please tell him to go and buy some breakfast.
ช่วย บอก เขา ให้ไป ซื้อ อาหาร เช้า ด้วย
tʃûuai *bɔ̀ɔk-kháu-hâi* pai sɯ́ɯ aahăan-tʃáau dûuai
please *tell-he-make* go buy food-morning also

- **bɔ̀ɔk-kháu-hâi** บอก เขา ให้ *to tell him*
- here the object, **kháu** คุณ *him*, is placed between the verb **bɔ̀ɔk** บอก *to tell* and **hâi** ให้

2.1 A different word order

Please tell him to go and buy some breakfast.
ช่วย บอก ให้ เขา ไป ซื้อ อาหาร เช้า ด้วย
tʃûuai *bɔ̀ɔk-hâi-kháu* pai sɯ́ɯ aahăan-tʃáau dûuai
please *tell-make-he* go buy food-morning also

- **bɔ̀ɔk-hâi-kháu** บอก ให้ เขา *to tell him*
- **hâi** ให้ can also be placed before the object, **kháu** คุณ *him*
- the meaning here is the same as in the above sentence, **bɔ̀ɔk-kháu-hâi** บอก เขา ให้ *to tell him*
- it depends on the speaker and perhaps also on the context which structure is used

3. Warn everybody – tuuan-thúk-khon-hâi...
เตือน ทุกคน ให้...

We must warn everybody that that place is very dangerous.

เรา ต้อง เตือน ทุก คน ให้ รู้ ว่า ที่ นั่น อันตราย มาก
rau tông *tuuan-thúk-khon-hâi* rúu wâa thîi-nân antàraai mâak
we must *warn every-person-let* know that place that dangerous very

- **tuuan-thúk-khon-hâi** เตือน ทุก คน ให้ *to warn everybody*
- the object, **thúk-khon** *everybody,* is placed here between the verb **tuuan** เตือน *to warn* and **hâi** ให้

3.1 A different word order

We must warn everybody that that place is very dangerous.

เรา ต้อง เตือน ให้ ทุก คน รู้ ว่า ที่ นั่น อันตราย มาก
rau tông *tuuan-hâi-thúk-khon* rúu wâa thîi-nân antàraai mâak
we must *warn-let-every-person* know place that dangerous very

- **tuuan-hâi-thúk-khon** เตือน ให้ ทุก คน *to warn everybody*
- **hâi** ให้ may be also placed before the object, **thúk-khon** *everybody*
- the meaning here is the same as in the above sentence, **tuuan-hâi-thúk-khon** เตือน ให้ ทุก คน *to warn everybody*
- it depends on the speaker and perhaps also on the context which structure is used

Secret 22 – hâi ให้ and changing the word order

B. Understanding hâi ให้ and changing the word order

Usually, when the position of **hâi** ให้ is changed in the sentence, the meaning of the sentence is also changed.

Here we demonstrate that in some cases **hâi** ให้ can be placed before or after the object, and the meaning remains the same. However, the colour of the statement can be sligtly different.

For example, when using the verb **bɔ̀ɔk** บอก *to tell*, **hâi** ให้ can be placed after or before the object as follows:

Word order

> *bɔ̀ɔk-kháu-hâi* + verb or *bɔ̀ɔk-hâi-kháu* + verb
>
> *tell-make-he* + go = tell him to go

Examples:

> Tell him to go to buy breakfast.
> บอก เขา ให้ ไป ซื้อ อาหาร เช้า
> *bɔ̀ɔk-kháu-hâi pai sɯ́ɯ aahǎan-tʃáau*
> *tell-he-make* go buy food-morning

- here **hâi** ให้ is placed after the object, here **kháu** เขา *him*

Different word order:

Earlier we have demonstrated (Secrets 6–9) how **hâi** ให้ as a compound verb was used as the second element in the compound structure as follows:

> *bɔ̀ɔk-hâi-kháu*+ verb...
>
> *tell-make-he* + go = tell him to go

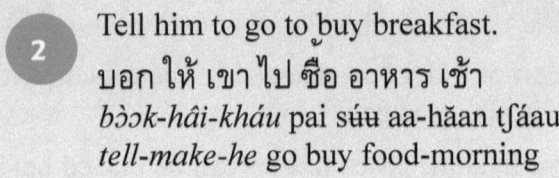

> **2** Tell him to go to buy breakfast.
> บอก ให้ เขา ไป ซื้อ อาหาร เช้า
> *bɔ̀ɔk-hâi-kháu* pai sɯ́ɯ aa-hǎan tʃáau
> *tell-make-he go buy food-morning*

- here the verb **hâi** ให้ is placed directly after the verb, **bɔ̀ɔk** บอก *to tell*

- this structure has been used in Secrets 6–9. Note that the meaning of these two statements 1 and 2 is the same. It depends on the person, which structure is used

- however note that the structure in the sentence 1, *tell-him-hâi* + go is not possible with all verbs

Conclusion
Sometimes changing the word order, placing the object (pronoun) between the other verb and **hâi** ให้ is fine, and other times it is not possible. See more about this in *Language hints* and in *Simple advice* in this Secret.

C. Language hints

With some verbs the word order can be changed

The most common verbs are:

khɔ̌ɔ	ขอ	*to ask*
tʃəən	เชิญ	*to invite*
bɔ̀ɔk	บอก	*to tell*
sàng	สั่ง	*to order, to request*
tɯɯan	เตือน	*to warn*
rîiak	เรียก	*to call, to call out*
athíbaai	อธิบาย	*to explain*
tsɛ̂ɛng	แจ้ง	*to inform*

Secret 22 – hâi ให้ and changing the word order

a) Both of the following sentences are right and have the same meaning.

Examples:

> **1**
> I invite you to go with me.
> ฉัน เชิญ ให้ คุณ ไป ด้วย
> tʃán *tʃəən-hâi-khun* pai dûuai
> I *invite-make-you* go together

- this structure is commonly used by Thais
- this structure can be used with all verbs
- **hâi** ให้ is placed directly after the first verb, here **tʃəən** เชิญ *to invite* and before the pronoun, here **khun** คุณ *you*

> **1.1**
> I invite you to go with me.
> ฉัน เชิญ คุณ ให้ ไป ด้วย
> tʃán *tʃəən-khun-hâi* pai dûuai
> I *invite-you-make* go together

- this structure cannot be used with all verbs. See the section b) below.
- with this verb the word order may be changed, and the pronoun **khun** คุณ *you* is placed between the verb **tʃəən** เชิญ *to invite* and **hâi** ให้
- it depends on the speaker which structure is used, 1 or 1.1

b) With some verbs the word order cannot be changed:

Secret 22 – hâi ให้ and changing the word order

> **1** **Warning**
> It is not correct to say:
> I want him to go to buy breakfast.
> อยาก เขา ให้ ไป ซื้อ อาหาร เช้า
> *yàak* kháu *hâi* pai súu aahăan-tʃáau
> *want* he *request* go buy food-morning

- **yàak** อยาก *to want* cannot be followed by a noun or a pronoun. It always need to be followed by a verb
- hence it needs to be followed by **hâi** ให้ *to let* or another verb

> **1.1** Correct!
> I want him to go to buy breakfast.
> อยาก ให้ เขา ไป ซื้อ อาหาร เช้า
> *yàak-hâi-kháu* pai súu aahăan-tʃáau
> *want-request-he* go buy food-morning

- here **yàak** อยาก *to want* is followed by the verb **hâi** ให้, and this is correct

> **2** **Warning**
> It is not correct to say:
> I need you to move a little.
> ผม ต้องการ คุณ ให้ ขยับ หน่อย
> phŏm *tôŋ-kaan* khun *hâi* khàyàp nòi
> I *require* you *request* move little

- in this sentence the verb **tôŋ-kaan** ต้องการ and **hâi** ให้ cannot be separated

Secret 22 – hâi ให้ and changing the word order

2.1 Correct!

I need you to move a little.

ผม ต้องการ ให้ คุณ ขยับ หน่อย
phǒm *tông-kaan-hâi-khun* khàyàp nòi
I *require-request-you* move little

- here **hâi** ให้ follows directly the verb **tông-kaan** ต้องการ *to need*
- that is correct and sounds good

3 It is not correct to say: **Warning**

He allowed me to go on the trip.

เขา ยอม ฉัน ให้ ไป เที่ยว
kháu *yɔɔm-tɕǎn-hâi* pai thîiau
he *allow-I-let* go trip

- the verb **yɔɔm** ยอม *to allow* and **hâi** ให้ cannot be separated here

3.1 Correct!

He allowed me to go on the trip.

เขา ยอม ให้ ฉัน ไป เที่ยว
kháu *yɔɔm-hâi-tɕǎn* pai thîiau
he *allow-let-I* go trip

- **yɔɔm-hâi** ยอม ให้ *to let, to allow, to permit* is a compound verb
- these two verbs **yɔɔm** ยอม and **hâi** ให้ must go together here as used in this sentence

D. Simple advice

Every language is unique and special in its own way. For instance, if you say in English *Tomorrow I go to school,* every native English speaker would know that you should in fact say *Tomorrow I am going to school*. Why? Perhaps there isn't any simple easy explanation available. These particular structures have been born by using the language for hundreds of years.

To know when the word order can be changed in Thai, and when it cannot, you almost need to be a native speaker to have a feeling for this. This is one of those specialities of the Thai language that non-native speakers find difficult.

If in doubt use the word order as follows and as explained in Secrets 7–11.

bɔ̀ɔk-hâi-kháu + *verb*

Tell-request-he + go = Tell him to go

> Tell him to go to buy breakfast.
> บอก ให้ เขา ไป ซื้อ อาหาร เช้า
> *bɔ̀ɔk-hâi-kháu pai súɯ aa-hǎan tʃáau*
> *tell-make-he* go buy food-morning

- in this structure, **hâi** ให้ is placed directly after the first verb, here **bɔ̀ɔk** บอก *to tell* and before the pronoun, here **kháu** เขา *he*
- using this structure is always right no matter which verb we are using

The aim of this book has been to teach you how to speak Thai as Thai people do using the verb **hâi** ให้. We have given some grammatical and common sense explanations as much as possible given the scope of this book.

PART VI

Introduction to Thai sounds
and some useful grammar terms

A. Introduction to sounds and Thai transliteration

Many western students think that it is too difficult to learn to read Thai letters and do not invest the time and effort to learn them. It is true that you do not need to have a command of the Thai writing system in order to speak Thai. However, if you can master at least the basics of the Thai writing system, it will be a big help for your studies. It makes sense, therefore, to learn the Thai characters from the beginning.

Western letters can only be used as an aid in learning to speak Thai. You should not use western letters in writing Thai sentences. There are so many different ways to transliterate that your effort would be fruitless. Thais would be unlikely to understand what you had written. In Thailand, western letters are only used in names and road signs.

Western letters may aid your understanding of how certain Thai words are pronounced, but if you do take the trouble to learn to read and write the Thai script, Thai people will be very impressed!

Note that we do not review the tones in this section. We give, however, the correct tone symbols in transliterations. We transliterate Thai sounds with western letters or international phonetic symbols. This process is called phonetic writing, transliteration and sometimes also romanization.

This presentation includes all consonant and vowel sounds used in central Thai. However, there are many more Thai consonants, and also some vowel sounds can be written in several different ways.

In Thai there are all together 20 consonant sounds and 18 pure vowel sounds.

By knowing how new sounds are made both in theory and practice, you will become more confident in learning Thai. Then practise and adjust your speaking until you can make new sounds correctly.

If in doubt, please review this section and also read the book *22 Secrets of Learning Thai – Complete Guide to Sounds, Tones and Thai Writing System*.

1. Thai consonant sounds

Many foreign words borrowed from Pali, Sanskrit or Khmer use rare consonants for common sounds. Hence, in the Thai alphabet list, 42 consonants make only 20 different consonant sounds.

Basically, there are three types of consonant sounds in Thai, namely stop consonant sounds, fricative consonant sounds and sonorant consonant sounds. This distinction is very important in Thai in order to understand the Thai writing system and tones.

1.1 Stop consonant sounds

Stop consonant sounds can be divided into four basic categories, namely aspirated consonants, unaspirated consonants, affricate consonants and voiced consonants.

1.1.1 Aspirated stop consonants

Aspiration means that there is a puff of air coming out of your mouth when you produce the sound. Stop consonants are produced in such a way that air is first stopped by the lips or by the tongue and then released by a plosive.

phɔɔ พ, **th**ɔɔ ท, **kh**ɔɔ ค

- the letter **h** is used to denote the fact that the sound is aspirated with the puff of air

Thai words:

phaan	พาน	*tray*
phûŋ	ผึ้ง	*bee*
phɛɛŋ	แพง	*expensive*
tháhǎan	ทหาร	*soldier*
thǔŋ	ถุง	*bag*
thêep	เทพ	*God*
khwaai	ควาย	*water buffalo*
khài	ไข่	*egg*
khon	คน	*person*

Similar English sounds: **P**eter, **p**erson, **p**aper, **t**ime, **t**ake, **t**one, **k**iss, **k**ey, **k**eep

Rating: Good

- these sounds are not difficult for English speakers since similar consonant sounds in English are always aspirated at the beginning of a word or a syllable
- put your hand in front of the mouth, and feel that there is a puff of air coming when you say these words either in Thai or in English

1.1.2 Unaspirated stop consonants

When the sound is unaspirated, it means that there isn't any puff of air coming out of your mouth when you produce this sound. The sound is first stopped by the lips or by the tongue and then released in such a way, that there is no any puff of air coming out of your mouth when you make this consonant sound. The air is somehow stopped in the glottis. This is called in phonetic terms a glottal stop.

pɔɔ ป, **t**ɔɔ ต, **k**ɔɔ ก

Thai words:

plaa	ปลา	*fish*
pìt	ปิด	*to close*
pìip	ปีบ	*cork tree*
tàu	เต่า	*turtle*
tên	เต้น	*to dance*
tiin	ตีน	*foot* (not polite)
kài	ไก่	*chicken*
kɛ̀	แกะ	*to unwrap*
kɛ̀ɛ	แก่	*to be old*

Similar English sounds: s**p**eak, s**p**ell, s**p**y, s**t**op, s**t**ink, s**t**ate, s**k**in, s**k**ate, s**k**y

Rating: Not very good

- the tricky point is that in English we don't have unaspirated consonant sounds at the beginning of a word or a syllable

- we have therefore taken as examples similar consonant sounds in the middle of the word where the English aspiration is weak
- put your hand in front of the mouth, and make sure that there is no puff of air coming when you say these Thai words
- you may need some practice before getting the pronunciation of these words right without any puff of air. Do no hesitate to consult your Thai teacher

1.1.3 Affricate stop consonants

Affricate consonant sounds consist of two sounds at the beginning of the word, **tʃ** or **ts**. They can be either aspirated or unaspirated.

These affricate stop consonant sounds are produced in such a way that the air is first stopped by the tongue and then released.

tʃɔɔ ช and tsɔɔ จ

In Thai there are two affricate stop consonant sounds, **tʃ** as in the word **tʃɔ̂ɔp** ชอบ and **ts** as in the word **tsing** จริง. The first sound in Thai is aspirated, and the second is unaspirated. English also has two affricate sounds, **tʃ** as in the word **ch**ild and **dʒ** as in the **j**ob. The first sound in English is aspirated, and the second is voiced.

English stop sounds at the beginning of a word are usually divided into aspirated and voiced. In Thai, the similar initial sounds are aspirated or unaspirated.

tʃɔɔ ช

Thai words:
tʃáang	ช้าง	*elephant*
tʃing	ฉิง	*cymbals*
tʃɛ̌ɛ	แฉ	*to reveal, to show*

Similar English sounds: **ch**ild, **ch**oose, **ch**apter

Rating: Good

- with this sound English speakers usually don't have any problem

- you may use the English sound and there should not be any problem
- put your hand in front of the mouth, and feel that there is a puff of air coming when you say these words either in Thai or in English

tsɔɔ จ

The sound **tsɔɔ จ** is perhaps the most misunderstood Thai sound among non-native speakers. Therefore, we try to explain it here in detail.

This Thai sound **tsɔɔ จ** is transliterated in many ways, examples include: **j, ch, c, dsch**. The most correct way to transliterate this sound would be to use the international phonetic symbol **tɕ**. It is not known very well however and therefore seldom used. We have decided to use simply **ts**.

Thai words:

tsaan	จาน	*plate*
tsùm	จุ่ม	*to dip*
tsùu	จู่	*to rush*

Similar English sounds for **tsɔɔ จ**: **g**in, **j**oy, **ts**unami

Rating: Not very good

- the letter **j**, as in the English word **j**oy, is often given as an example. This is, however, not quite right, since the English consonant **j** is voiced, but the Thai sound **ts จ** is unvoiced
- note that if you pronounce the word **ts**unami as it is written and not like **s**unami, you are close
- make sure that you start with **t**-sound and then glide into **s**-sound. Put your hand in front of the mouth, and feel that there is not much air coming from your mouth when you say the above Thai words
- note also that English sounds, which are not aspirated at the beginning of the word are usually voiced. This Thai sound **tsɔɔ จ** is not voiced, not aspirated but unaspirated

- **ts**unami is a foreign word and is pronounced in several different ways by English speakers and therefore it is not a very good example
- the same type of foreign sound is the Russian word **ts**ar
- why is this sound difficult for English speakers? The reason is because there is no such a sound at the beginning of English words. The same sound exists frequently at the end of the word in English. Good examples are: Le**t's**, ca**ts**, ha**ts**, bi**ts** etc...
- note, however, if you pronounce this sound as in the English word **j**ob, you will be understood by Thais since there is no similar voiced sound in Thai for it to be confused with. In that case your pronunciation is not quite correct

1.1.4 Voiced stop consonants

Voiced sounds in Thai and in English are not aspirated. They are produced in such a way that vocal folds are vibrating. The sound is first stopped by the lips or by the tongue and then released.

bɔɔ บ, **d**ɔɔ ด

Thai words:

bai máai	ใบ ไม้	*leaf*
bin	บิน	*to fly*
bìip	บีบ	*to squeeze*
dèk	เด็ก	*child*
dù	ดุ	*to scold*
duu	ดู	*to look, to see*
din	ดิน	*land, earth*

Similar English sounds: **b**aby, **b**anana, **b**ig, **d**inner, **d**uck, **d**ance

Rating: Good

- here there is no problem at all. The English sounds are very similar to the Thai sounds

- note, however, that at the beginning of a word or a syllable the consonant sounds in English are either voiced or aspirated, but in Thai they can be aspirated, unaspirated and also voiced

1.2. Fricative consonant sounds

Fricative consonant sounds are produced in such a way that the air is not stopped but directed through a narrow channel. The turbulent airflow makes a friction. In Thai there are only two fricative sounds, namely **f** and **s**. Fricative consonants sounds in Thai are unvoiced.

In English there are three fricative sounds, **f, s** and **z**. In Thai the voiced counterpart **z** does not exist.

In order to be complete, we need to add one more fricative sound, the glottal fricative sound **h**, which is used similarly in Thai and in English.

fɔɔ ฟ, ซ sɔɔ, hɔɔ ฮ

Thai words:

fan	ฟัน	teeth
fǎa	ฝา	lid, cover
fǔung	ฝูง	group, flock
sôo	โซ่	chain
sǔua	เสือ	tiger
sǔun	ศูนย์	zero
nók hûuk	นกฮูก	owl
hìip	หีบ	chest
hɛ̂ɛng	แห้ง	dry

Similar English sounds: **five, fax, form, seven, simple, same, he, have, host**

Rating: Good

- if you use the English pronunciation for these three sounds, there should be no problems

1.3. Sonorant consonant sounds

The term sonorant sound means that the sound can be prolonged without any difficulty. The sound is not stopped by lips or by tongue. Sonorant sounds play a very important role as far as the Thai writing system is concerned. They are:

mɔɔ ม, **n**ɔɔ น, **l**ɔɔ ล, **r**ɔɔ ร, **ng**ɔɔ ง, **y**ɔɔ ย and **w**ɔɔ ว

Most sonorant sounds are pronounced in a similar way in Thai and in English

If you use the English pronunciation for the following sonorant consonant sounds, there should be no problems.

There are, however, two sounds that we would like to explain in more detail, namely **r**ɔɔ ร and **ng**ɔɔ ง

mɔɔ ม

Thai words:
máa	ม้า	*horse*
mǎu	เหมา	*to presume, to rent*
mâai	ม่าย	*widow*

Similar English sounds: **m**other, **m**ake, **m**ain

Rating: Good

nɔɔ น

nǔu	หนู	*mouse*
nâu	เน่า	*rotten*
nǎau	หนาว	*cold*

Similar English sounds: **n**ine, **n**ice, **n**ot

Rating: Good

lɔɔ ล

ling	ลิง	*monkey*
lǎi	ไหล	*flow*
lǎai	หลาย	*many*

Similar English sounds: **l**ine, **l**ips, **l**oose

Rating: Good

rɔɔ ร

Thai words:

rʉʉa	เรือ	*boat*
rai	ไร	*something*
raai	ราย	*item*

Similar English sounds: **r**ed, **r**ead, **r**ipe

Rating: Not very good

- many Thai speakers substitute this **r** ร-sound with the **l** ล-sound as in the English world like. So, it is quite common that Thai is spoken without the correct Thai **r** ร-sound
- when the correct **r** ร-sound is used by Thais, it is not exactly the same sound as the English **r**-sound
- Thai **r** is rolled more like the Spanish **r**
- some English speakers may produce this sound differently depending on origin of the country, education etc...

ngɔɔ ง

Thai words:

nguu	งู	*snake*
ngong	งง	*to be confused*
ngóong	โง้ง	*to be bent*

English words: ki**ng**, si**ng**ing, fi**ng**er

Rating: Not very good

- this sound **ng** ง appears in several combinations in the English language
- however, it can prove quite difficult for English speaking learners to use this sound at the beginning of a word. This shows how strongly language skills are based on habits
- you may practise this sound by saying the first part of the word si**ng**ing silently and the second part loudly

yák	ยักษ์	*giant*
yím	ยิม	*smile*
yîiam	เยี่ยม	*excellent*

Similar English sounds: **y**ellow, **y**es, **y**ear

Rating: Good

wɛ̌ɛn	แหวน	*ring*
wai	ไว	*fast*
wǎai	หวาย	*wicker palm*

Similar English sounds: **w**omen, **w**ife, **w**inter

Rating: Good

2. Thai vowel sounds

In Thai there are 9 short and 9 long pure vowel sounds. With these 18 vowel sounds you will be able to make all Thai vowel sounds including diphthongs and all other vowel combinations.

The main obstacle with the Thai vowel sounds for English speakers is to learn to separate short vowel sounds from their long counterparts. In Thai vowels are produced clearly short or long.

In English the pronunciation of vowels can vary depending on the person and the accent. Often in English the short vowels can be prolonged or long vowels shortened without loosing the meaning of the word. This can't be done with Thai vowels.

Note also that when we transliterate the vowel sounds, we write a short sound with one symbol and a long sound with two symbols. Some transliteration systems do not separate short and long vowels. Then there is no way to know how to pronounce those vowels. If you don't pronounce Thai vowels clearly, Thai people will have difficulty to understand you.

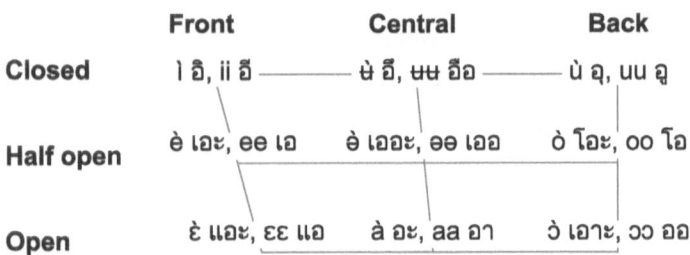

ì อิ and ii อี

Learn to separate the short **ì อิ**-sound from its long counterpart **ii อี**.

Thai words:

bì	บิ	to break off
bìip	บีบ	to squeeze, to press
pìt	ปิด	to close
pìip	ปีบ	cork tree
bin	บิน	to fly
biin	บีน	(only a sound, no meaning)

Similar English sounds for short **ì อิ**: h**i**ppy, th**i**nk, s**i**t

Similar English sounds for long **ii อี**: s**ee**, m**ea**t, t**ea**ch

Rating: Good

- if you use the English pronunciation for the short **ì อิ** and long **ii อี** sound, there should be no problems
- just make sure that the short sound is short and the long sound clearly long
- note also that some English speakers, particularly Americans, tend to make this sound towards **e**-sound as in the English word p**e**t

ʉ อึ and ʉʉ อือ

Learn to separate the short **ʉ อึ**-sound from its long counterpart **ʉʉ อือ**.

Thai vowel sounds

It is often said that there is no comparable sound in English for these two sounds. This is not quite true, since some English speakers, even in England and USA, seem to use a similar sound with words like c**ou**ld, sh**ou**ld, g**oo**d, c**u**te, f**ew** and r**u**de. Others pronounce the same sound differently.

Thai words:

phùng	ผึ่ง	*to dry, to expose*
phùun	ผืน	*prickly*
bûng	บึ้ง	*to be serious*
pûun	ปื้น	*eruption on the skin*
phûng	ผึ้ง	*bee*
phǔun	ผืน	*sheet*

Similar English sounds for short ʉ อึ: sh**ou**ld, g**oo**d, w**ou**ld

Similar English sounds for long ʉʉ อือ: c**u**te, f**ew**, r**u**de

Rating: Not good

- listen to the audio CD and try to adjust your sound to conform with the Thai sound
- if you are facing difficulties, we would advise you to find a good native Thai teacher to get this sound right since you can't directly use the English sounds
- remember to make a short sound short and a long vowel sound clearly long

ù อุ and uu อู

Note that the long English **uu** อู-sound is sometimes pronounced differently by different English speakers. Some may use a version similar to the Thai sound, **ʉʉ** อือ. This happens often with words like n**ew**, d**ew**, g**oo**d, t**wo**.

Do not mix up these two sounds **ù** อุ and **ʉ** อึ or **uu** อู and **ʉʉ** อือ. In Thai, they are clearly different sounds. In English, the distinction is not so clear.

Thai words:

fùn	ฝุ่น	dust
fǔung	ฝูง	group
pù	ปุ	to repair
pùu	ปู่	grandfather
bun	บุญ	merit
phuun	พูน	to pile up

Similar English sounds for short **ù** อุ: l**oo**k, p**u**t, f**oo**t

Similar English sounds for long **uu** อู: c**oo**l, s**oo**n, d**o**

Rating: Quite good, but pay attention

- do not mix up the short **ù** อุ with the short **ʉ** อึ
- do not mix up the long **uu** อู with the long **ʉʉ** อือ
- they are made in a similar way. **ù** อุ and **uu** อู are made with rounded lips and **ʉ** อึ and **ʉʉ** อือ are made with unrounded lips

è เอะ and ee เอ

The short **è** เอะ and the long **ee** เอ-sounds do not exist in their pure form in Standard English.

Thai words:

thét	เท็จ	false, incorrect
thêet	เทศ	foreign
pen	เป็น	to be
pheen	เพล	lunch time (monk)
pèt	เป็ด	duck
thêep	เทพ	god, divine being

Similar English sounds for short **è** เอะ: p**e**t, s**ai**d, br**ea**d

Rating: Quite good, but pay attention

Similar English words for long **ee** เอ: p**a**le, p**ai**nt, s**ai**l

Rating: Not very good

- some English speakers pronounce the short **è** เอะ sound in English close to the Thai sound **ɛ** แอะ while others may pronounce it differently

- note that in Thai vowel sounds can't be changed in any way. They need to be pronounced clearly

- the long **ee** เอ sound doesn't exist in its pure form in Standard English

- if you pronounce the **ee** เอ sound as in the English word p**a**le like p**ee**l without the **i**-sound, you are close to this Thai sound

- listen to the audio CD and ask your native Thai teacher to correct your pronunciation in order to learn to get these two sounds exactly right

ə̀ เออะ **and** əə เออ

Learn to separate this short ə̀ เออะ-sound from its long counterpart əə เออ.

These two sounds appear in English often with the consonant **r**. In order to get the Thai sound right you should not pronounce the **r**-sound.

Thai words:

də̂n	เดิ้น	*smart* (slang)
dəən	เดิน	*to walk*
tə̀	เตอะ	*(only a sound, no meaning)*
təəm	เติม	*to fill, to add*
bə̀ng	เบิ่ง	*to look* (Isaan dialect)
pə̀ət	เปิด	*to open*

Similar English sounds for short ə̀ เออะ: ab**ou**t, teach**er**, **A**nglia

Similar English sounds for long əə เออ: h**er**, b**ir**d, b**ur**n

Rating: Quite good, but pay attention

- if you speak American English, please be aware that you should pronounce short **ə̀ เออะ** and long **əə เออ**-sounds without the **r**-sound. If in doubt, ask your native teacher to help you get these sounds exactly right

ò โอะ **and oo** โอ

Be aware that in Thai, long and short vowels are pronounced the same, only the duration is different. These two sounds in English are usually turned into a vowel combination such as **ou** or **əu**.

Please make sure that you are able to understand and produce these sounds correctly. You need to learn to make these sounds, short and long, without the u-sound.

Thai words:

son	ซน	*to be naughty*
soon	โซน	*zone, area*
sòt	สด	*fresh*
sòot	โสด	*single, unmarried*
tòt	ตด	*to fart*
dòot	โดด	*to jump*

Similar English sounds for short **ò** โอะ: folk, roll, bolt

Similar English sounds for long **oo** โอ: g**o**, hell**o**, l**a**w

Rating: Not very good

- the short **ò** โอะ and the long **oo** โอ sounds do not exist in their pure form in Standard English
- for the short **ò** โอะ sound you need to learn to say the English word **folk**, without the **ù** อุ-sound
- for the long **oo** โอ you must learn to say the English word *go* without the **ù** อุ-sound as g**oo**
- make this long **oo** โอ-sound longer than the short **ò** โอะ. It is close to the long **ɔɔ** ออ-sound as in the English word **law**

ɛ̀ แอะ and ɛɛ แอ

Learn to separate the short ɛ̀ แอะ-sound from its long counterpart ɛɛ แอ.

Thai words:

tʃɛ̀	แฉะ	wet
tʃɛ̄ɛ	แฉ	to reveal, to show
tsɛ̀	แจะ	sound of chewing
tsɛ̀ɛk	แจก	to hand out
kɛ̀	แกะ	to unwrap
kɛ̀ɛ	แก่	to be old

Similar English sounds for short ɛ̀ แอะ: cat, hang, at

Similar English sounds for long ɛɛ แอ: sad, bad, mad

Rating: Quite good, but pay attention

- if you use the English sound as in the word **cat** for the short ɛ̀ แอะ- sound, you are quite close

- if you use the English sound as in the word **bad** the long ɛɛ แอ, you are quite close

- Note, however, that some English speakers tend to pronounce the long ɛɛ แอ as in the English word **bad** shorter than it is pronounced in Thai. Make sure that you always pronounce long vowel sounds long in Thai.

à อะ and aa อา

Note that in Thai, it is very important to maintain the correct length of a vowel. When the vowel length changes, the meaning of the word changes as well. In English the length of the vowel can be changed without loosing the meaning.

Thai words:

khâ	ค่ะ	ending particle
khâa	ค่า	*price*
kàt	กัด	*to bite*
kàat	กาด	*market* (Northern dialect)
khát	คัด	*to select, to copy*
khàat	ขาด	*to be missing*

Similar English sounds for short **à** อะ: b**u**t, r**u**n, fl**oo**d

Rating: Good

Similar English sounds for long **aa** อา: f**a**ther, v**a**st, p**a**ssport

Rating: Quite good, but pay attention

- for the short Thai **à** อะ sound the English sound may be used without any difficulty as in the word r**u**n

- however, some English speakers, particularly Americans, tend to pronounce the long **aa** อา-sound similar to the sound in the English word s**a**d, written phonetically as sεεd. They tend to say pεεsport instead of **paa**sport. You need to be careful not to change the quality of the sound when you produce these short and long vowels in Thai

- listen to the audio CD and then check with your native Thai teacher so that you can pronounce these two sounds clearly and exactly right

ɔ̀ เอาะ **and** ɔɔ ออ

Learn to distinguish the short ɔ̀ เอาะ-sound from its long counterpart ɔɔ ออ. Note that in Thai the difference between long and short vowel is only the length of the sound.

In English, however, changing the length of the vowel sound makes often qualitatively different sound as it is the case with these two sounds.

You also need to learn to distinguish ɔ̀ เอาะ and ɔɔ ออ from ò โอะ and oo โอ. Even though these sounds are quite close, you need to learn to hear, understand and reproduce the difference.

Thai words:

hông hông	ห้อง	*room*
hɔ̌ɔm	หอม	*to smell*
hông-gong	ฮ่องกง	*Hong Kong*
hɔ̀ɔ	ห่อ	*package*
tông	ต้อง	*must*
thɔ́ɔng	ท้อง	*stomach*

Similar English sounds for short ɔ เอาะ: **not**, **got**, **soft**

Rating: Not very good

Similar English sounds for long ɔɔ ออ: **all**, **caught**, **law**

Rating: Quite good

- standard English does not have the short ɔ เอาะ-sound in its pure form

- one way to explain the short ɔ เอาะ-sound is to use the long ɔɔ ออ-sound as in the word **law** but make it short. You may need help from a native teacher to get this sound right

- if you make the long ɔɔ ออ-sound as in the English word **law**, you will be quite close. In Thai, this vowel is perhaps pronounced more open than the similar vowel sound in English. More open means that you open your mouth a bit more

- do not mix up these two sounds, short ɔ เอาะ and short o โอะ

- do not mix up these two sounds, long ɔɔ ออ and long **oo** โอ

- they are made in the similar way

∽

B. Summary of some useful grammar terms

I. Grammar

In every language, we need to be able to make sounds in such a way that other people understand what we are saying. We also need to be able to put words together in such a way that sentences make sense and sound right. As an adult learner, this requires some conscious and active effort on your part.

When you are learning a second language as a child, you are growing into it. Learning a second language as an adult is a different process. The learning process is not that intuitive any more. Your brain also wants to understand what you are learning. If the correct way is not readily available to you, your brain will understand things in its own way. In other words, it makes assumptions, right or wrong, from point of view of your own native language. Since Thai uses a different kind of syntax to English, the assumptions made may not be valid. You need to think the way Thai people do in order to speak Thai fluently.

1.1 Phonetics

Phonetics is concerned with the sounds of the language. This is quite important since English sounds cannot be directly transferred into Thai. This is true particularly with the vowel sounds. If you want to be understood by Thais, you need to be able to produce correct Thai sounds.

See more about how Thai words are pronounced in the section "Introduction to Thai sounds and transliteration" (pages 267–285). You can also find more comprehensive explanation of Thai sounds in the book *22 Secrets of Learning Thai – Complete Guide to Sounds, Tones and Thai Writing System*.

1.2 Transliteration

Transliteration is a way to write Thai sounds with western letters and international phonetic symbols. This helps you to get sounds right since it may take a long time for you to able to read the Thai script properly. See more about the transliteration of Thai sounds at the end of this book.

1.3 Syntax

Syntax is concerned with the structure of the language, how the words are put together in the sentence. This is important since the Thai language uses a different type of syntax from English.

1.4 Semantics

Semantics is concerned with the meaning of words and sentences. This is important since one word can have several different semantic meanings. **hâi** ให้ is a very good example of this type of word. It may change the semantic meaning when placed in different positions in a sentence.

1.5 Semantic boundary

We use the term *semantic boundary* to describe the fact that we need to use different English words in order to define the meaning of the verb **hâi** ให้. We need to use English words such as *to give, to let, to make, to order* etc. to grasp the correct meaning of **hâi** ให้. See the section "B. Conclusion" in each Secret of this book.

> ## 2. Parts of speech
> When describing the structure of the Thai language, we need to know a few basic terms, usually called in English *parts of speech*.

2.1 Nouns

2.1.1 Common nouns

The word *common noun* is a word used for things such as *dogs, cats, cars, computers*. They have a physical form and they can be touched. **hâi** ให้ can be placed before a noun in order to have a distinct meaning, *to give*. See Secret 1.

2.1.2 Abstract nouns

An *abstract noun* is a word used for things like *luck, beauty* and *effectiveness*. These nouns do not have a physical form and cannot be touched. **hâi** ให้ can be placed before an abstract noun in order to have a distinct meaning. See Secret 2.

2.1.3 Classifiers

Thai count nouns are called *classifiers*. In English we also have classifiers: *two bottles of milk, head of cattle, a class of beer*. Perhaps, more accurate term for this type of nouns is "measure words". The difference is that in Thai it is compulsory to use classifiers for all nouns when counting. For example, you cannot say in Thai *two cars*. You must say *a car two vehicles*. *Vehicle* would be here a classifier in Thai. **hâi** ให้ can be placed before a classifier in order to have a distinct meaning.

2.2 Personal pronouns

Personal pronouns such as *I, he* and *we*. In Thai personal pronouns are used much more and in a wider sense than in English. They refer to age, gender, social status and the context. **hâi** ให้ can be placed before a personal pronoun in order to have a distinct meaning, *to let* or *make* someone do something. See Secret 4.

2.3 Verbs

2.3.1 Main verb

When **hâi** ให้ is a *main verb*, it means *to give*. See Secrets 1–3.

2.3.2 Helping verb

As a *helping verb* **hâi** ให้ is placed before the main verb or after it. When hâi ให้ is placed before a main verb, then it is usually understood as a causative verb, *to make* someone do something.

2.3.3 Action verbs

Action verbs are verbs that express actions like *to run, to work, to dance*.

2.3.4 State verbs

State verbs describe a state that usually lasts for some time. Some common examples where the state is described are: *to be (He is tall), to have (I have fever), to feel (I feel good).*

2.3.5 Causative verbs

Causative verbs are commonly used in English and in Thai. Causative verbs cause or make something happen. **hâi** ให้ is commonly used as a causative verb or a *causative compound* verb in Thai. Some common causative verbs in English are: *to let, to make, to have.* See Secret 4.

2.3.6 Causative compound verbs

Causative compound verbs are used frequently in Thai in the sense that two verbs together form a new meaning. **hâi** ให้ is commonly used as compound verb with many other verbs. When using the compound verb in Thai, the structure is quite tight. This means that we usually cannot put other words between the two verbs. See Secrets 5–8. Using compound verbs in this way is very rare in English. **hâi** ให้ can also be placed directly after another verb in order to have a distinct meaning. See Secret 9.

2.4. Adjectives

2.4.1 Adjectives as adjectives

Adjectives in Thai can be used as *adjectives* as we understand them in English. Adjectives usually answer the question "what kind?". Example: *good, beautiful, happy.* **hâi** ให้ can be placed directly before an adjective in order to make an adjective become an adverb. See Secret 14.

2.4.2 Adjectives as verbs

Adjectives in Thai can be used as *verbs*. In Thai, an adjective can play the role of the English verb *to be.* For the sentence to be complete, all you need is a subject and an adjective. There is no need for any verb as such. A similar structure is not possible in English.

2.4.3 Adjectives as adverbs

Adjectives in Thai can be used as *adverbs*. In Thai adjectives can play the role of an adverb of manner. In Thai when an adjective follows an action verb, "good" becomes *well*, "beautiful" becomes *beautifully* and "slow" becomes *slowly*.

2.5 Adverbs

2.5.1 Adverbs of time

Adverbs of time tell us *when* an action happened, will happen or perhaps that it is happening now. Examples: *yesterday, two days ago, tomorrow, nowadays*.

2.5.2 Adverbs of frequency

Adverbs of frequency are used to tell us *how often* the action happens. Examples: *often, regularly, always*.

2.5.3 Adverbs of place

Adverbs of place are used to tell us *where* the action happens. Examples: *far, near*.

2.5.4 Adverbs of manner

Adverbs of manner are used to tell us *how and in what way* the action happens. Examples: *slowly, well, gently*. See Secret 15. **hâi** ให้ can be placed directly before an adverb in order to have a distinct meaning.

2.6. Prepositions

Both Thai and English use *prepositions* like *in, to, above, for*. In Thai the verb **hâi** ให้ can also be used as a preposition. When **hâi** ให้ is placed before a pronoun and after the main verb, it is best translated into English as the preposition *for (for you, for me, etc.)* See Secret 13.

2.7 Conjunctions

Conjunction words such as *and, or, but, until* are used to connect two sentences. In Thai the verb **hâi** ให้ can be used as the conjunction word *until*. See Secret 16.

Summary of some useful grammar terms

3. Making sentences

In oder to make correct sentences, there are a few basic English terms which may prove helpful to know while learning Thai.

3.1 Simple subjec

The *simple subject* is a *noun* or a *pronoun*. It is a person or thing that actively performs an action, the one who is in charge.

3.2 Simple predicate

The *simple predicate* is a *verb*, which describes or tells something about the subject. In Thai an adjective can be both a predicate and an adjective at the same time. No separate verb, as we understand it in English, is needed.

3.3 Object

3.3.1 Direct object

The term *direct object* is used for something which is given.

3.3.2 Indirect object

The term *indirect object* is used for the person to whom the direct object is given.

3.4 Subject-verb-object in the sentence

As you will learn in this book, the subject or the object can be dropped in Thai if understood from the context. For example, the sentence *I'll give it to you* can be expressed as *give*. See Secrets 1–3.

3.5 Tenses

The term *tense* in English is used to describe time aspects such as *past, present* and *future*. The semantic meaning of the word tense is that the verb changes form when different tenses are used in English.

The grammar rules in Thai are very straightforward. For instance, the verbs are not conjugated, there are no tenses for verbs, there are no plural forms for nouns and no genders or articles like *a, an* or *the*.

3.6 Time aspect

In Thai the *time aspect* (past, present, future) is made clear by *words* while in English it is made clear by *tenses and words* (example: *I went yesterday to...*). Sometimes, we conveniently use the English word *tense* to talk about the Thai *time aspect*. We may say this is a past tense in Thai, even though there are no tenses in Thai as such. So, please do not get stuck with the definition of the English word *tense*. After all we are taking about the past, present or future whether we call it a tense or a time aspect.

3.7 Context

Context can be *verbal* or *social* or both. We use the word *context* in this book in a sense that the speaker takes into account the surroundings in which the conversation takes place and adapts her or his language to suit that context. Therefore, much maybe already understood and not everything needs to be spoken out.

3.8 Short form

We use the *short form* in the sense that when the context is clear, some words, which can be understood from the context, are dropped or left out.

3.9 Idiomatic expressions

Idiomatic expressions are informal ways to convey meanings. An idiomatic phrase may have a different meaning than the words in it. **hâi** ให้ is used in many idiomatic expressions in Thai. Idiomatic expressions give some juice to the expression. See Secret 17.

3.10 Gerund

Gerund is a grammatical term used in English for nouns that are formed from verbs by the ending *-ing* such as *giving*. This kind of noun (gerund) can be a subject or an object in a sentence. In Thai, we form nouns from verbs by placing the prefix **gaan** การ before the verb. **gaan-hâi** การให้ is translated into English as *giving*.

3.11 Genitive/possessive case

The term *genitive* is used to show *possession*. In English it is usually formed by adding *'s* after a noun or by placing the word *of* before the noun. In Thai the possessive form is created by the word **kɔ̌ɔng** ของ *of*. See more about how to form "genitive" in Thai in Secret 9 "C. Language hints".

3.12 Polite particles

In Thai *polite particles* are used frequently. The most common are **khâ** ค่ะ and **khráp** ครับ. They are not very easy to translate into English. Therefore, we have not given an exact English translation for them in our "word for word" translations. The overall meaning is close to the English word *please*. The Polite particles in Thai are used grammatically a different way to the English word *please*. Their usage and "semantic boundaries" are much wider. See Secrets 10–12.

4. Other terms

4.1 Schwa

Even though the *schwa* is a most common vowel sound in English, this term is not usually known by native speakers of English language since phonetics is not commonly taught in schools while spelling is. The schwa is a short neutral vowel sound used in English. The sound depends on the consonant it is attached to. A good example is the letter "a" in the word *about*. However, the same letter is pronounced very differently in words such as *can, sad, make, article* where it is not the schwa. The vowel sounds are very clear and distinct in Thai and they cannot be blurred or changed to anything else like schwa in English.

∾

Bibliography

Becker, Benjawan Poomsan. *Thai for Beginners.* Paiboon Publishing, California, 1995.

Becker, Benjawan Poomsan. *Thai for Intermediate Learners.* Paiboon Publishing, California, 1998.

Becker, Benjawan Poomsan. *Thai for Advanced Learners.* Paiboon Publishing, California, 2000.

Burusphat Somsonge. *Reading and Writing Thai.* Institute of Language and Culture for Rural Development, Mahidol University, Bangkok, 2006.

Dhyan, Manik. *22 Secrets of Learning Thai – Complete Guide to Sounds, Tones and Thai Writing System*, Dolphin Books, 2014.

Higbie, James & Thinsan Snea. *Thai Reference Grammar: The Structure of Spoken Thai.* Orchid Press, Bangkok, 2003.

James, Helen. *Thai Reference Grammar.* D.K. Editions & Suk's Editions, Bangkok, 2001.

Kanchanawan, Nitaya & Eynon, Matthew J. *Learning Thai (A Unique and Practical Approach).* Odeon Store, Bangkok, 2005.

Ponmanee, Sriwilai. *Speaking Thai for Advanced Learner.* Thai Studies Center. Chiang Mai Universtity, Chiang Mai, 2001.

Professor Dr. Wit Thiengburanathum. *Se-Ed's Modern Thai-English Dictionary Mini Edition*, Bangkok 2011.

Smyth, David. Thai: *An Essential Grammar.* Routledge, London and New York, 2002.

Smyth, David. *Teach Yourself Thai.* Hodder Headline, London, 2003.

Thampusana-Abold, Tipawan. *Thai for English Speaking Learners. Grammatical and Cultural Approaches.* D.K Editions & Suk's Editions, Bangkok, 1995.

* * *

Our books can be obtained from the following bookshops in Thailand:

DK today
www.dktoday.co.th

Asia Books
www.asiabooks.com

Kinokuniya
www.kinokuniya.com

Chulalongkorn University Book Center
www.chulabook.com

Thammasat University Bookstore
www.bookstore.tu.ac.th

Chiang Mai University Bookstore
http://www.cmubook.com

Naiin Bookstore
www.naiin.com

Sounds of the Thai Language Basic Sounds

Book I – Secrets 1–15

ISBN 978-9526651323, 182 pages

Sounds of the Thai Language (Book I) teaches you all the basic sounds used in spoken and written Thai. It includes 20 consonant sounds and 18 pure vowel sounds. It points out the main obstacles for learners, for example which Thai sounds are most difficult for an English speaker to produce. It then gives you handy tips to help overcome these difficulties. Much care has been taken to describe each sound in phonetic as well as in practical terms so that everyone should be able to grasp the correct way to produce Thai sounds.

The book has been designed so that it can be used by all levels of Thai learners. It contains a special exercise section, which teaches you in a step by step manner how to learn to read Thai script.

The book includes MP3 download spoken by native speakers to give you examples of how the words are produced in practice. In addition to individual words, the audio features many of the most common expressions used by Thai people in everyday conversation. This book is suitable for self-study and can also be used as an aid in the classroom. It contains a vast number of tips to assist you in learning Thai and understanding some of the crucial cultural aspects of the language.

This book and audio will set you on the road to confident Thai language learning.

Sounds of the Thai Language
Advanced Sounds

Book II – Secrets 16–22

ISBN 978-9526651330, 178 pages

Book II teaches you the advanced sounds of the Thai language such as consonant clusters, rare consonants, vowel combinations, final sounds and tones rules.

It includes the audio file spoken by native speakers to give you examples of how the special words are pronounced in practice. In addition to individual words, the audio features many of the most common expressions used by Thai people in everyday conversation.

This book is suitable for self-study and can also be used as an aid in the classroom. It contains a vast number of tips to assist you in learning Thai and understanding some of the crucial cultural aspects of the language. This book and audio will set you on the road to confident Thai language learning.

If you are a beginner, it is recommended that you first read Book I – Basic sounds. It gives you an overall understanding of the basic sounds used in spoken and written Thai and includes all 20 consonant sounds and 18 pure vowel sounds.

Much care has been taken to describe each sound in phonetic as well as in practical terms so that everyone should be able to grasp the correct way to produce Thai sounds.

The free MP3 audio files can be downloaded from the address: www.thaibooks.net

Learning Thai with hâi ให้

ISBN 978-9526651156, 296 pages

hâi ให้, along with words like dâai ได้, lέεu แล้ว and kɔ̂ɔ ก็, is one of the most important words in the Thai language.

When speaking Thai, it is important to understand the correct usage of the verb hâi ให้ in everyday speech.

One simple way to use the verb hâi ให้ is *to give something to someone*. It is used in a similar manner as the English verb *to give*.

In addition, hâi ให้ is used as a causative verb which has several different meanings depending on the situation, and the way it is spoken. It can be translated into English as *to let, to allow, to make* and even *to order* or *to force someone to do something*.

In some situations hâi ให้ is better translated into English as the preposition *for*, as in *for you, for me*, etc. It is also often used in idiomatic phrases where it carries no meaning itself but denotes only the sense of a command.

Thais use the verb hâi ให้ in an intuitive way in a variety of situations in order to express feelings, wishes, commands and nuances of meaning while communicating with each other every day.

If you learn this word well, you will be rewarded.

Learning Thai with dâai ได้

Book I – Secrets 1–14

ISBN 978-9526651200, 283 pages

Whether you are a beginner or an advanced learner, you certainly want to learn to speak Thai fluently. This book will take you a long way towards your goal.

dâai ได้ is one of the most common words in Thai. It is a multifunctional helping verb and is used by Thais in several different ways. It has many distinct meanings depending on where it is placed in a sentence and which other words are used with it. With this book you won't just learn how to use dâai ได้ but will also acquire a deeper knowledge of the Thai language in general.

Included are:

- complete and informative written examples
- audio spoken by native speakers
- highlights and explanations of dâai's ได้ usage
- sections of simple and easy to understand advice
- useful hints and tips on dâai ได้ and the spoken Thai language

Furthermore, you will get to see the language "through the eyes of dâai ได้". Study this book and you will be rewarded; your Thai friends will be amazed at your deep understanding of the subtleties of their language.

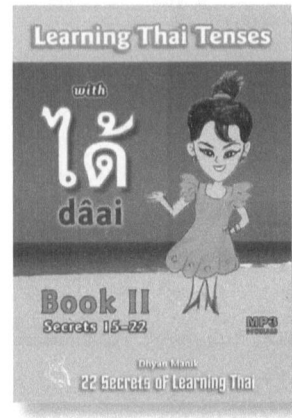

Learning Thai Tenses with dâai ได้

Book II – Secrets 15–22

ISBN 978-9526651408 , 278 pages

Whether you are a beginner or an advanced learner, you will surely want to learn to speak Thai fluently. In order to do this, it is vital to use time words and tense markers correctly.

The English term *tense* is also a handy way to talk about past, present and future activities in Thai, even though there are no *tenses* as such in the Thai language. When compared to English, Thai tenses are expressed very differently.

It is often said that dâai ได้ denotes a past tense. However, it would be better not to think of dâai ได้ as the past tense marker since it can also be used to refer to present or future events.

To help you speak Thai fluently the Book II includes:
- complete and informative written examples
- audio spoken by native speakers
- highlights and explanations of dâai's ได้ usage
- sections of simple and easy to understand advice
- useful hints and tips on dâai ได้ and the spoken Thai language

Books I and II complement each other. However, each book has a different focus. In Book I, Secrets 1–14, we introduced dâai ได้ and explained where it should be placed in sentences. dâai ได้ has several grammatical functions; hence, it also has several meanings depending on the context. In Book II, Secrets 15–22, we focus on tenses.

Have fun while you study them both; then, you will understand how Thais express themselves in everyday life!

Learning Thai with Original Thai Words

ISBN 978-9526651439, 320 pages

Do you want to learn to speak Thai as naturally as Thais do? Thai is not as difficult as you may think! If you follow the guidelines of this book, you will acquire a basic knowledge of the language in just a few weeks.

Students, usually, face several obstacles when studying Thai. In this book, we shall explain clearly what these obstacles are and how to overcome them. We shall also point out what you need to know and what you may ignore when learning to speak Thai. This will ensure your time and effort is focused on the things that really matter. You will be in a position to make an informed decision on how to proceed and deepen your language skills.

We use a simple and direct method which is easy to comprehend. You don't have to master the complex Thai writing system in order to speak Thai fluently. In this book, we concentrate on "original Thai words" which form a very important part of the Thai vocabulary and are used by Thais every day in conversation.

The book is designed in such a way that it can be used by both beginners and by those who have already reached intermediate level.

Included are:

• written examples and sentences • audio spoken by native speakers • highlights, explanations and examples on "how the language works" • simple and easy to understand advice • hints and tips on spoken Thai language • "Take it further" section which includes many more tips on how to proceed with your studies

Now, you can tell all your friends that learning Thai can be easy. Read this book and you will discover how!

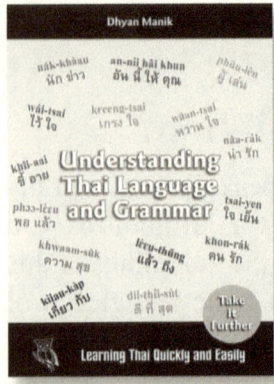

Understanding Thai Language and Grammar

ISBN 978-9526651460, 264 pages

Understanding the structure and grammar of the Thai languge is very important since it may differ considerably from your own language

Included are:
- Original Thai words compared to foreign origin words
- Personal pronouns and family members
- Days, weeks, months, seasons and numbers
- Telling time – 24-hour clock compared to the Thai style
- Foods, drinks and spices
- Travelling, places, buildings and countries of the world
- Names of animals and insects
- Health words and personal items
- Adjectives, adverbs and verbs
- Thai question words, prepositions and conjunction words
- Classifiers and prefixes
- tsai ใจ heart -word
- Summary of the Thai tenses
- Words of wisdom

Learning Thai Quickly and Easily

– Learning Thai with Original Thai Words (2019)
– Learning Thai Language and Grammar (2020)
– Learning Thai with English Words (coming 2024)
– ABC of Thai Language and Grammar (coming 2025)
– Learning Thai with Foreign Words – Pali, Sanskrit, Khmer, Chinese... (coming 2026)

22 Secrets of Learning Thai

– Learning Thai with hâi ให้ (2016)
– Learning Thai with dâai ได้ Book I, Secrets 1–14 (2018)
– Learning Thai Tenses with dâai ได้ Book II, Secrets 15–22 (2018)
– Sounds of the Thai Language Book I – Basic Sounds, Secrets 1–15 (2020)
– Sounds of the Thai Language Book II – Advanced Sounds, Secrets 16–22 (2021)
– Mastering Thai Grammar and Tenses with lɛ́ɛu แล้ว Book I, Secrets 1–7 (2023)
– Mastering Thai Grammar and Conjunction Words with lɛ́ɛu แล้ว Book II, Secrets 8–11 (coming 2024)
– Mastering Thai Language and Grammar with lɛ́ɛu แล้ว and Her Friends Book III, Secrets 12–22 (coming 2026)
– Learning Thai with kɔ̂ɔ ก็ (coming 2027)

For more information

www.thaibooks.net
www.facebook.com/22secrets

www.ingramcontent.com/pod-product-compliance
Lightning Source LLC
LaVergne TN
LVHW091627070526
838199LV00044B/964